Abigail Bray is an autonomous writer (and lifelong vegetarian) who lives in the South of France. Dr Bray has held research positions at universities in Australia and has published numerous peer-reviewed articles on embodiment, violence, moral panics and sexualisation. Her last book was *Big Porn Inc: Exposing the Harms of the Global Pornography Industry* (Spinifex, 2011) edited with Melinda Tankard Reist. She is an inaugural inductee in the U.N.-sponsored Western Australian Women's Hall of Fame.

Other books by Abigail Bray

Hélène Cixous: Writing and Sexual Difference (2004)

Body Talk: A Power Guide for Girls (2005)
with Elizabeth Reid Boyd

Big Porn Inc: Exposing the Harms of the Global Pornography Industry (2011) with Melinda Tankard Reist

MISOGYNY RE-LOADED

Abigail Bray

First published by Spinifex Press 2013
Spinifex Press Pty Ltd
504 Queensberry St
North Melbourne, Victoria 3051
Australia
women@spinifexpress.com.au
www.spinifexpress.com.au

Editors: Susan Hawthorne and Renate Klein
Copy editor: Maree Hawken
Cover design: Deb Snibson
Typesetting: Palmer Higgs
Typeset in Bembo and Futura
Indexer: Karen Gillen
Printed by McPherson's Printing Group

National Library of Australia
Cataloguing-in-Publication data:

Bray, Abigail, 1966–   author.
Misogyny re-loaded / Abigail Bray.

9781876756901 (paperback)
9781742195476 (ebook : epub)
Includes bibliographical references and index.
Misogyny.
Women in popular culture.
Feminine beauty (Aesthetics).
Human body—Social aspects.
Women—Social life and customs.
Women—Social conditions.
Women—Violence against.
Man–woman relationships.
305.4

 This project has been assisted by the Australian Government through
the Australia Council for the Arts, its arts funding and advisory body.

PEFC
PEFC/21-31-16

Contents

1.0 The Fascism That Has No Name

They made it clear from the start that the slightest deviation from the norm would be punished. They turned everything into prisons, even our own bodies.

Wear pink. Play with dolls. Look in the mirror. Go to school. Learn to smile when they abuse you. Diet, wax, apply make-up, and swallow your medication. Follow fashion. Work. Consume. Be silent. Give him a porn star experience. Get married. Shop, cook, wash, iron, dust, vacuum, scrub and polish. Work a 15-hour shift (but don't call housework 'work'). Get into debt. Have children. Stay married (or they'll destroy you and your children). Watch TV. Wear stilettos. Obey their laws. Save for your old age. Now repeat after me: 'I am free'.

Just to make sure I knew who my masters were they spat on me, groped me, pinched me, grabbed me and shoved me at school, in the street, in homes, on buses, in parks, pubs, clubs, everywhere. They shouted at me from cars, building sites, pub windows and doors, everywhere that I was a slut, an ugly bitch, a fat slag, a stupid cow, a skinny cow, a sexy dog, that they would fuck me, hit me, damage me, and destroy me. They made grunting noises and flapped their tongues. They raped me, beat me, pulled the hair out of my head, and kicked me. They threatened to kill me and told me to kill myself. They always wanted to know my weight, size, age and height as though this information was useful for their plans. They harassed me when I studied or worked, they just wouldn't leave me alone. Then they told me I lacked a sense of humour.

I had nightmares about them and was afraid to walk the streets at night.

"Get over it," they said. (But how can you get over something that never stops?)

When I spoke about it they said I had a 'victim mentality' and I needed to move on and let go of the past. Often the past they spoke about was a few hours ago, yesterday, or the week before.

"You are too sensitive," they said. "You can choose to move on from your disempowering negative attitude. Be compassionate, practise forgiveness." They said, "You are 110% responsible for everything that happens in your life, and you have no one to blame but yourself. (You know you want it.)"

They told me to forget all about the historical oppression of women because they got that sorted in the 1970s. They told me all of this even though I could still remember the day when I was a child and I discovered that the word 'girl' was an insult. Girl. The inferior sex. The more she grows the more her inferiority shows itself in her body.

I carved their hatred into my skin, I overdosed on their hate and starved my body with a hundred diets because I did what they told me to, and I took it personally. They said, "We have pills to help you take responsibility for your life. Do yourself a favour, give yourself a chance, you have a chemical imbalance in your brain." They threatened me with electric shock therapy when I refused their pills.

They said, "A woman is nothing without a man. Never admit to being treated badly by a man or we will punish you. Get married and be cruel to single women. Stay married because we destroy single mothers."

They said I was stupid so I studied for seven years and got a PhD. Afterwards they said, "You think too much, stop thinking, you talk too much, stop talking." When I disagreed with them they asked me if my period was due. They sniggered, sneered, rolled their eyes, laughed, and turned their backs. When I spoke they pretended I didn't exist.

They came up to me in the street and asked me why I wasn't smiling. "Smile!" they shouted at me, "it makes you look pretty!"

They told me I needed to pay a therapist to teach me how to be normal. I asked her if she thought there might be a power imbalance between the sexes and she looked at me silently for five minutes. Then she said, sighing with impatience, "It's not about him it's about you. How do you feel? What have you done to invite this situation into your life?" I said, "Listen I didn't start this, they've been coming after me since I was a kid, I can't seem to shake them off, they're everywhere, they even seem to have control of the media and the government." She said I sounded paranoid, that I might be having a psychotic split from reality and offered to have me committed. I said, "Have you heard of something called the women's liberation movement?"

Year after year I watched the women and girls around me taking it personally, and in desperation telling each other to take it personally. They turned against each other and fought over men, clothes, handbags, shoes, rings, washing machines, haircuts, couches, bras, the shape of each other's bodies, housework, children, jobs. They dieted, did a bit of bulimia on the side, stabbed each other in the back, took up pole dancing, had burlesque parties, did a bit of home-made porn, took antidepressants, and boasted about how loved they were by the men who oppressed them.

They played me heterosexual love songs in supermarkets and boutiques, on radio stations and TV. They said, "Listen … this is the love that is waiting for you if you obey us." They said, "Play hard to get, and don't talk back or we'll call you a bunny boiler." Then they said, "From now on you must pay a stranger to pour boiling wax all over your vulva and rip out your pubic hairs on a regular basis. Don't complain about it. Have your breasts, face, vagina, and ass redesigned with knives and implants. Put it on your credit card. Pretend you enjoy rough anal sex or we will call you frigid and boring. Here," they said, "read *The Rules*. It's only natural, biological, and an evolutionary truth." I said, "This is getting very weird." They winked at me and in a silky seductive sexy voice they said, "Hey listen babe you just need to have fun." I said, "Your heterofascist entertainment rituals bore me to death."

They told me to practise positive thinking and cleanse myself of toxic negative emotions. They told me to live in the 'Now' like a toddler, or a goldfish with a five-second memory. They treated me like a child, demanded that I behave like a child and look like a 15-year-old, and then they told me I was immature and childish.

They said, "Consider yourself lucky, this is a democracy and we've given women the freedom to choose their own lives and be what they want to be."

When I mentioned the word 'misogyny' they called me a man-hater. When I spoke up against fascist pornography they told me I needed a good fuck. "The answer to your problems," they said, "is between our legs." When I spoke about the rise of rape culture they told me I definitely needed a good fuck. But by then I had stopped taking it personally.

"Listen," I said, "what we really need is a vigorous, earth-shaking, relentless, uninhibited, wild, passionate, intoxicating, angry, unapologetic, long-overdue, exciting, luscious *revolution*."

Because this was never personal, this was always political.

▽ ▽ ▽

Wake up, sister.

Patriarchal capitalism has you.[1]

It is the system that has been pulled over your eyes to blind you from the truth.

What you know you can't explain, but you feel it. You've felt it your entire life, that there's something wrong with the world. You don't know what it is, but it's there, like a splinter in your mind, driving you mad.

I know why you find it hard to sleep at night. You are terrified. Sometimes you speak about it but no one listens to you. You were born into bondage. You are a slave among slaves. Look around you. What do you see? Lawyers, housewives, academics, secretaries, shop assistants, people so reliant on the system that they will defend it. That system is our enemy. It is destroying the planet. The laboratory of advanced patriarchal capitalism has created the monster of austerity fascism and it is stalking us all. The riot police are spreading across the world; beating women, children, and the old. Debt bondage is increasing, unemployment escalating. Rape culture is on the rise, prostitution is mainstreamed. The minds of the children have been poisoned.

> There was a time when you were not a slave, remember that …
> You say there are no words to describe this time, you say it does
> not exist. But remember. Make an effort to remember. Or, failing
> that, invent.
>
> —Monique Wittig, *Les Guérillères* (1972, p. 95)

---

1   See *The Matrix* (1999): "Wake up Neo; the matrix has you"; and "The Matrix is a system, Neo. That system is our enemy. But when you're inside, you look around, what do you see? Businessmen, teachers, lawyers, carpenters. The very minds of the people we are trying to save. But until we do, these people are still a part of that system and that makes them our enemy. You have to understand, most of these people are not ready to be unplugged. And many of them are so inert, so hopelessly dependent on the system that they will fight to protect it."

Sometime in the 1980s the global pornography industry went viral. By 2000 a new genre became popular called 'gore' or 'snuff'.[2] Photographs and videos of people being murdered and dying, their body parts hacked up and their brains spilling out of their skulls became a form of mass entertainment. They plugged everyone in, even the children. Websites celebrating the destruction of women began to saturate the net. They told us to call it 'pornography'. It became fashionable to masturbate and laugh at the annihilation of women. Destroying women became the slapstick lulz[3] of the new sexual fascism.

We were warned this would happen but we didn't do enough. We were afraid of losing our jobs, of being called 'man-haters', of being cast out. We were unable to create solidarity with one another, we didn't yet know how to trust each other, we called each other 'victim feminists', we lost ourselves in petty squabbles, and now it is almost too late.

▽ ▽ ▽

In 2012 I interviewed the scholar and activist Jeffrey Masson about his involvement in the anti-pornography movement in the 1990s. During our conversation he mentioned that anti-pornography feminists in that era were aware of the existence of 'snuff pornography' and went on to speculate, quite reasonably, about the growth of the snuff pornography market. Intellectually, I could accept that this was possible given the aggressive increase in hardcore pornography over the last

2   The few articles on 'gore' typically ignore the blatant fact that these websites are soaked in hardcore pornography and are brutally misogynistic. For an example of the disappearing of women see <http://mybroadband.co.za/news/internet/82429-arrests-in-canadian-psycho-film-case.html> and also <http://www.theverge.com/2012/6/13/3076557/snuff-murder-torture-internet-people-who-watch-it> (accessed 21 July 2013).

3   "'Lulz' is how trolls keep score. A corruption of 'LOL' or 'laugh out loud,' 'lulz' means the joy of disrupting another's emotional equilibrium" (Schwartz, 3 August 2008).

few decades. I had seen more hardcore pornography than most women, and knew how mainstream it was. But emotionally, I could not imagine or comprehend that human beings were being filmed while they were being raped and slaughtered or that this kind of 'pornography' might have increased. I was so disturbed by Masson's insistence that snuff existed that I put the interview into a drawer, telling myself I would write it up later.

Three months later I would meet a professional man in his late thirties who confessed that he had been watching these websites for many years. He didn't call what he watched 'snuff pornography'; he simply said that he sometimes watched hardcore websites with videos of people being killed. I asked him why he watched this kind of material and his answer chilled me: he said it was funny, that it made him feel alive, and that he watched it when he felt bored.

1.1 Welcome to the Extermination Camps

> Most of you know what it means when 100 corpses lie there, or when 500 lie there, or when 1,000 corpses lie there. To have gone through this and—apart from a few exceptions caused by human weakness—to have remained decent, that has made us great. That is a page of glory in our history which has never been written and which will never be written.
>
> —Heinrich Himmler's speech (4 October 1943)

Masson was right. 'Snuff pornography'—photographs and filmed footage of women and girls being tortured, raped and murdered—not only exists, it even has numerous Facebook Inc. fan clubs. It is time we recognised the casual normalisation of lethal misogyny as an act of political terrorism and not, as the mindless purveyors of the free speech doctrine would argue, as simply the democratic right to masturbate to whatever takes *his* fancy.

The Young News Channel (YNC) is merely one of countless 'gore' social media websites that distribute many thousands of pornographic photographs and videos of dying and dead women.[4] The majority of these websites also promote violent rape, bestiality and incest. They have names such as 'deadskirts', 'femme fatalities', 'femme gore', 'dead nude women', '2kill4', and advertise with words such as "girls butchered, executed or viscously brutalized in every conceivable way." One popular gore or snuff website advertises itself with an image of an "Asian woman roasted on a spit over a fire like a pig" and features sections on "sexual disasters" and carries advertisements for hardcore pornography websites. The image of the impaled woman is possibly a reference to the 1980 Italian snuff film *Cannibal Holocaust* in which a girl is gang-raped and impaled.[5] The website has around 15 million views a month and is operated by Mark Marek, a Holocaust denier who was arrested for distributing a video made by former prostitute Luka Magnotta which features dismemberment, necrophilia and cannibalism.[6] Luka Magnotta and his snuff porn video have cult status.

---

4   YNC can be easily accessed on Facebook Inc. and YouTube: the presence of snuff in social media is normalised. Far from being 'underground' or hidden within the inaccessible regions of the 'dark web', pornographic images of dead and dying women are mainstream and available for peer-to-peer exchange. I have met several men who have confessed to seeing snuff pornography involving a man being dismembered by another man and anally penetrated while dead. Indeed this snuff video went viral. See <http://mybroadband.co.za/news/internet/82429-arrests-in-canadian-psycho-film-case.html> (accessed 21 July 2013). The men I have spoken to are reluctant to discuss the circulation of images of butchered and raped dead women in the gore social networks that are connected to the hardcore pornography matrix.

5   See Rose (15 September 2011).

6   See <http://news.nationalpost.com/2013/08/01/website-owner-charged-over-graphic-video-at-centre-of-luka-magnotta-case-gets-bail-second-time/> (accessed 7 August 2013).

Is it naïve to argue that this is as fictional as a splatter film? Or, to cite the 1976 film *Snuff* that appeared to feature a girl being savagely raped, murdered and dismembered but which the producers claimed was fake? *Snuff* was pre-Internet and before smart phones made it possible to film anything and anyone and distribute it anonymously online or through peer-to-peer networks. There is police evidence that child sexual abuse material, in which children are killed, exists.[7] And if we know this, why do we think snuff pornography involving women does not exist?[8] There are countless places in the world where women have no substantive rights, are sold as sex slaves, and killed with impunity. Snuff videos are common, as a discussion on Sherdog.com (UFC, Mixed Martial Arts) about the 'deep web' puts it: "[T]here are snuff videos you can access—especially now that Mexican drug cartels are finding out you can record shit."[9] It is highly possible that snuff pornography exists in this context.

That pseudo-snuff pornography exists is clear. It would be naïve to trust that the men who distribute it are to be believed when they say it is merely staged 'play acting', as it were. Just as

7   See for example, Burke, Gentleman and Willan (1 October 2000) who quote a senior customs officer: "We have seen some very, very nasty stuff involving sadistic abuse of very young children, but actual deaths on film takes it a whole step further. That is very worrying."

8   The following is from an article which ridicules people who think that snuff pornography exists: "When porn-chic poster girl turned anti-porn crusader turned centerfold Linda Lovelace spoke before the U.S. Attorney General's Commission on Organized Crime, she included firsthand claims of genuine snuff rumors in her testimony. She revealed that women who were no longer useful to the porn industry were routinely murdered both on and off camera. But Lovelace, like all the other outraged voices, never produced hard evidence" <http://ww.fringeunderground.com/snuff.html> (accessed 21 July 2013).

9   'Have you heard of the deep web' <http://forums.sherdog.com/forums/f48/have-you-heard-deep-web-1577233/index15.html> (accessed 21 July 2013). The forum contains discussions where men confess to having seen girls and women murdered. Many gore websites contain member only sections and it is probable that the worst content is shared there.

it would be foolish to believe that the models in pseudo-child pornography are all 18 or older. Porn consumers who watch one video of a woman being tortured and raped followed by another of a girl lying butchered in a pool of blood are effectively watching snuff pornography. Can they, in fact, tell the difference?

The mocking of women in the process of being butchered, the overt celebration of not merely sexual violence against women but the kind of violence that results in the slaughtering of women, indicates that we have entered a new era of misogynistic hate. Consider, for example, if there were thousands of websites on the net promoting the death of Jewish people. We would have no hesitation in recognising a political alignment with a pervasive history of anti-Semitism that resulted in the atrocities of the Holocaust. And yet, while racism is recognised as a form of hate speech, misogyny continues to be normalised and acceptable.

The snuff porn Facebook Inc. page and YouTube channel The Young News Channel is not only legal: it is a source of humour, a form of entertainment. The YNC advertises itself with the following words: "daily media, humour, shocking videos, rape videos, slaughter, disturbing videos." On the left-hand side of the homepage there is a list of categories. They are as follows: Sick daddy porn 18+, suicide 18+ only, hard core porn, murder video 18+, dead girls, female suicides, banned media, sick videos, rape. There are many hardcore porn images of girls being penetrated by horses and dogs, double anal penetration, images of a man's hands pulling open a woman's gaping ass, of disembowelled naked women in morgues with their legs spread, of disfigured naked women lying in pools of blood. The website is like a slaughterhouse, only there are women instead of animals.

On the homepage there is an advert for snuff pornography: "Image: HORROR. Beautiful Swedish model raped and murdered ..." And there is also "SHOCKING lunatic butchers mother and her baby with a meat cleaver in the street in public." Another section advertises "Underground video. Boyfriend convinces girlfriend to blow her brains out." Yet another offers viewers the chance to see "girl's brains fall out of her helmet as she is moved off the road." A video is promoted with the following words: "skirt in suicide ... teen female in nice skirt hanged herself from the HIGHEST tree." There is a photograph of a young girl hanging from a tree by her neck wearing a short skirt.

How do I bear witness to this atrocity, to women who have been destroyed, and after death have their destruction circulated as entertainment? And it is not merely entertainment; it is more akin to the way the KKK circulated photographs of lynched human beings as trophies (Hawthorne, 2011). It is hard to understand this—language reaches a limit, my mind feels stunned, silent; sociological and psychological explanations fall away.

The singularity of each death is obliterated, sinking into the larger mass of dead bodies. It's as though the websites were a death camp full of torture, rape, murder and suicide. What is this digital conveyor belt of dead women's bodies, this entertainment factory of mass death? Are these websites, to use Hannah Arendt's words about the Nazi death camps, "laboratories in the experiment of total domination" (1994, p. 240) of women?

It is important to recognise that this is occurring within the context of a sex war conducted against young women through social media and new communication technologies. It is now not uncommon to hear yet another news story of a teen girl who has been driven to suicide by online bullying, trolling, sexting, 'slut shaming' and prolonged abuse and social exclusion.[10] New communication technologies have intensified

---

10 See for example <http://www.dailymail.co.uk/news/article-2246896/Jessica-Laney-16-committed-suicide-internet-trolls-taunted-told-kill-herself.html> (accessed 6 August 2013).

and expanded misogyny so that smart phones have become political weapons, instruments of rape culture propaganda, in the hands of a population conditioned to secure their status within the group by practising hatred against girls and women.

YNC has a number of Facebook Inc. groups of various sizes, but the largest was established on 22 May 2011 and had 18,122 'likes' on 28 October 2012. In effect, 18,000 Facebook Inc. profiles had openly endorsed a website which distributes pornographic images of women being raped and slaughtered.

The 'About' section is blank. The cover shows Huynh Cong Ut's iconic 1972 black and white photograph of a naked nine-year-old Kim Phuc and other crying children running along a road in a futile attempt to escape a napalm attack on a Vietnamese village. There are several soldiers walking behind the children. Superimposed behind the soldiers where the dark clouds of napalm are rising is a grey YNC logo. By placing the YNC logo within the napalm clouds the group symbolically aligns itself with the United States military industrial complex and mocks the suffering of the children in this anti-war image. Indeed, many of the postings on the Facebook Inc. groups associated with YNC are little more than fascist celebrations of U.S. military imperialism. The profile picture is of a young white girl with a grotesque painted face in the style of the clown in the Stephen King film *It* (1990)—she is weeping blood. The contrast between the crying children and the smiling clown is sinister but one senses it is also intended to be amusing: it signifies the presence of sadistic lulz.

The wall posts are mostly monotonous soft-porn misogyny, photographs of young women with digitally enlarged breasts and asses, comments about using women as tables, 'slut shaming', and rape culture propaganda. There are also several photographs of cats. At a quick glance it seems like one of many thousands of Facebook Inc. groups that, under the cover of freedom of speech, function as popular propaganda outlets for misogyny. But there is one photograph that stands out. It has been taken at night.

▽ ▽ ▽

Consider if this is a woman
Without hair, without name
Without the strength to remember
Empty are her eyes, cold her womb.
—Primo Levi, *If This Is A Man* (2011, p. 17)

The photograph is of a slim young white woman wearing high-cut black shorts and a black top, sprawled in the kind of late night rubbish to be found spilling from inner-city street bins near nightclubs or pubs. Her bare legs are parted, and her head is on the curb of the pavement, next to an overflowing bin and partially turned away from the camera. The wide pool of blood seeping from her head has mixed with the rubbish. Underneath the photograph YNC fans have posted a few comments.

T.C. Le Blanc: 'haha the ync is the fuckn best dogg' (23 July 8.27 pm).
Michale Dollalute: 'yaa fuckin crazy night ...' (23 July 10.03 pm).
Even McMichael: 'Awe ... Someone threw away a perfectly good white chick. That just seems wasteful' (23 July 12.11 am).
Alice Janis: 'betcha she's dead' (9 August 1.13 am).
Alice Janis: 'and that blood comes from her head' (9 August 1.13 am).

'Alice's' assumption that the photograph is of a dead woman is not unreasonable. After all, the category 'dead girls' is clearly advertised on the homepage of the YNC.

There are no police or ambulances—the state has disappeared. There is only the silent, anonymous, invisible photographer, and a nameless bleeding dead girl lying in the rubbish on the side of the road. Her body has become human waste, something men "threw away" after a "crazy night."

Her death is also symbolic. Not only has this nameless dead girl quite literally been trashed, but so too has the idea that women have rights.

She has grown up in a culture where misogyny has been normalised, where the 'shock and awe tactics' of commercialised woman-hating are promoted as radical and rebellious. She has lived and died in a culture that is dominated by the ultra-conservative mainstream politics of sexual fascism.

Did she ever think, as a girl, that her dead body would become an image on the Facebook Inc. wall of a snuff pornography group promoting rape culture propaganda and killing women? Was her mother too afraid of being called a feminist man-hater to warn her daughter about the hatred of women?

This unnamed girl is the daughter of the backlash against second wave feminism. She is also part of a generation that, as Germaine Greer warned us in 1999 in *The Whole Woman*, were self-destructing in unprecedented numbers. She is part of a generation that Angela McRobbie argues suffers from lethal levels of self-hate that have become normalised since the backlash against second-wave feminism began during the 1980s. This generation of women, suggests McRobbie, endure the relentless abuses of intensified misogyny but have been robbed of a language and a politics through which to articulate their suffering. The loss of feminism, she writes, haunts them with a deep melancholia. Today, says McRobbie, many young women are "driven mad by a situation within which they now find themselves" (2009, p. 105).

The increase in eating disorders, self-mutilation, suicide, and other expressions of unbearable suffering among young women are a sign that radical new forms of misogyny are succeeding at destroying girls. In *The Whole Woman* Greer wrote that it is time to get angry again. Fourteen years later, we should be enraged. We inhabit an era in which misogyny is promoted as the new authoritarian *virtue* of an increasingly violent male-dominated culture.

There are occasional protests about the inclusion of footage of animal cruelty in Facebook Inc. groups—Gabe Blueburn Montoya writes: "I love death ... so pleasant ... I FUCKIN HATE ANIMAL CRULALTY [*sic*]" (25 July 2011, 11.32 am). Although the YNC Facebook Inc. groups incite racial hatred with, for example, overtly racist celebrations of the 'Collateral Murder' video[11] exposed by Private Bradley Manning via Wikileaks,[12] racism is also challenged. Tim Vidd writes: "[G]et those fucking idiotic retarded racists off your website cunt, it's annoying" (24 September 2012).

Is it not possible, after all, to celebrate and witness thousands of women being raped, tortured and murdered ... but remain sensitive about animals, and refuse racism? Have not some of these men, to recall Himmler's words, "remained decent"? Or perhaps, as Himmler implies, their decency, their humanity, is founded on the belief that women are sub-human, that they are *Untermenschen*? Because, to follow the long and violent logic of misogyny, the male body is the biological model of what counts as human. Animals have more value than women in these forums. This kind of misogyny is not the same thing as sexism: it is a form of fascism.

It is tempting to think of such men as members of a deviant subculture, a pathological underground, a sick minority. Yet splatter films which revel in pornographic scenes where women are tortured and killed are part of the mainstream; music videos celebrating male violence against women to the point of death and beyond are also mainstream. Misogynist hate propaganda is so normalised it has faded into the texture of the everyday— and we barely notice how pervasive it is. Consider the lyrics by Archive (British rock band) to songs such as 'Whore' (2010),

---

11 See <http://www.youtube.com/watch?v=5rXPrfnU3G0> for the 'Collateral Murder' leaked video (accessed 6 August 2013).

12 See <http://www.nydailynews.com/news/national/bradley-manning-defense-opens-baghdad-helicopter-shooting-video-article-1.1392937> (accessed 18 August 2013).

which is about shooting women who are breeding like swine, or their famous song, 'Fuck You' (2004),[13] about putting a gun in someone's mouth; or similarly a popular song by Vast (American rock band) called 'Pretty When You Cry' (1999) about sadistic sex with women. Or indeed the genre of death metal and of countless mainstream rap songs promoting the raping and killing of women. The fascist politics of misogyny have become the theme music of a new generation who have been brought up on hardcore porn.

During the 1990s, novels and films about serial killers became cool. Brett Easton Ellis's *American Psycho* (1991), in which a psychopathic upper-middle-class Wall Street broker rapes, tortures and murders women without remorse, has remained popular. I have met lawyers, and other professional Australian men who boast that they identified with the character in that film. Today in Australia the film *Chopper* (2000) and the television series *Underbelly* (2008), both of which feature psychopathic murderers who torture women, are popular with mainstream viewers. There is also the Australian classic *Wolf Creek* (2005), an example of how mainstream this genre has become.

The figure of the sexual psychopath appears to be a counter-cultural hero, the new old rebel, his ruthless sadism emblematic of a heroic masculinity which has transcended all those 'norms' which repressed his virile will to power. He emerges as the Nietzschean Superman, drenched in women's blood, surrounded by gore and a cold echoing laughter. Yet this new aspirational masculine ideal is distinctly conservative, he is one of the herd; as obedient and unreflective as the people who saluted Hitler for more than a decade.

---

13 Archive (2010) 'Whore' <http://www.youtube.com/watch?v=mpR_LaRQ RMI> (accessed 28 July 2013).
    Archive (2004) 'Fuck You' <http://www.azlyrics.com/lyrics/archive/fucku. html> and <http://www.youtube.com/watch?v=KfZpbWLl0Ew> (accessed 27 July 2013).

Lack of empathy towards women has not only been recoded as 'weak' or 'politically correct' or a sign that one is sympathetic to the 'f-word'—something worse has occurred. Cruelty towards women has become the leitmotif of a re-loaded misogyny that I have no hesitation in naming as fascist.

'Facial abuse'—or as the title further advertises: "extreme face fucking, deep rough gagging, mind fucking, facial abuse"—is on another porn website which celebrates the destruction of women. The terms of entry promise male viewers "graphic depictions of sexual passion so extreme that they will carry you away" and an "exciting and stimulating world of beauty and sex ... all emanating from the most essential, basic, and natural drives within each of us." The website denies that the content is "obscene" and states that "the legal right of adults to view these images is protected by our constitution" and that it is "accepted by every community in our nation." Although, it is admitted that it is "likely to offend or disturb some sensitive persons."

Or, to put it another way, the website argues that misogynist rape and sexual violence is the "most essential, basic and natural drive" of men and that the eroticisation of violence against women is a "legal right" for men. The use of the words "offend" and "disturb" along with "some sensitive people" have a hidden subtext: if one does not enjoy the website one is weak, feminine, of that class of (abnormally) sensitive people who suffer from being "offended" or "disturbed." Women's human rights have been obliterated. Masturbating to violence against women is an "essential, basic and natural drive" that is protected by the United States Constitution. Sex is collapsed with sexual abuse; misogyny with freedom of speech.

As Betty McLellan (2010) argues in *Unspeakable*, the ideology of 'free speech' is used to support the profit interests of the powerful over and against the oppressed. Writing about the issue of free speech and pornography Susan Hawthorne states, in no uncertain terms, that

[t]hose who promote the idea that pornography is about freeing our sexuality and maintaining free speech have betrayed their political roots. They are no longer on the side of the exploited and oppressed: they are instead supporting a massive capitalist venture which is based on humiliation, pain and exploitation. Just because those who are exploited are women does not mean that they should be regarded as having no human rights. Freedom is not a get-all-you-can menu. It is about justice and clarity, about who benefits and who loses (2011, p. 113).

The images on the homepage show bruised and bewildered girls' and women's faces splattered with semen. The website describes a girl who is assaulted until she becomes "unrecognisable," another who "turned blue from oxygen deprivation," yet another who has had her "dignity gagged out of her," and one who "just looked so broken," who has been "mentally and physically trashed."

These website *camps* can be understood as the core of misogyny; not an exception, but a barely disavowed norm. The logic of misogynistic extermination saturates the innumerable levels of social violence, of exclusions to the point of death, the bullying, psychological, economic and emotional violence that children and women endure in a male supremacist culture. The logic of misogynistic extermination runs through a criminal justice system which after almost half a century of attempted reform still blames women and girls for being raped, which colludes with rapists, paedophiles, women beaters and killers to re-abuse children and women when they seek justice. Children and women who have been beaten or raped by men are still considered 'damaged goods', their value as human beings diminished by male violence. Of girls and women in India who have been raped, it is said that their life is over; that they experience a commercial devaluation.[14] Yet orientalising the

---

14 See a discussion of the rape and murder of a young medical student in India <http://www.jadaliyya.com/pages/index/9371/orientalist-feminism-rears-its-head-in-india> (accessed 6 August 2013).

savagery of male supremacy does not take us very far; the same thing happens to females in westernised nations.

The silence and shame that cover up the misogynist abuse of women cannot be underestimated. Just as we have not yet understood how far this silence crushes women, we have yet to name the layers, the thousand plateaus, of male supremacist oppression.

Such websites are not only a symptom of the rising fascism of a new form of misogyny but also political attacks against feminism. They are being transmitted across the world in a context in which women's lives have become increasingly precarious. Naomi Klein's (2007) accurate assessment of the shock and awe tactics of 'disaster capitalism' is not just a theoretical possibility. Today we live in a world in which male supremacy is rapidly transforming into a form of global fascism, into what many are calling 'austerity fascism'. As feminist organisations are pointing out, women and children, *especially* women with children, are the most vulnerable to attack.

The necropolitical core of patriarchal capitalism is snuff pornography, the abject centre that no one wants to face. It is the logical conclusion of a system that treats women as 'things', of an irrational hatred which rapes and murders countless women every minute of the day simply because they are not male. We have entered the era of shock and awe misogyny.

1.2 Life that Does Not Deserve to Live

The worst survived—that is, the fittest; the best all died … These, and innumerable others, died not despite their valour but because of it … I must repeat—we, the survivors, are not the true witnesses … we are those who by their prevarications or abilities or good luck did not touch bottom. Those who did so … have not returned to tell about it or have returned mute, but they are the 'Muslims', the submerged, the complete witnesses, the ones whose depositions would have had a general significance.

—Primo Levi, *The Drowned and the Saved* (2003, pp. 64–65)

The Italian philosopher Georgio Agamben (1998) has argued that we must put Auschwitz at the centre of political and philosophical thought. His ideas are inspired by Primo Levi's autobiographical accounts of his experience in Auschwitz. Agamben's basic thesis is that the exterminatory logic of the Nazi death camps is not an exception to a norm; rather these death camps contain the disavowed secret of modern power. He argues, with chilling originality, that the biopolitical paradigm of modern power is the extermination camp, a laboratory of total domination in which human beings become sub-human, or *Untermenschen*. Killing those who have been labelled sub-human is not recognised as murder, an abuse of their human rights is not seen as abuse because they are no longer recognised as human beings.

The Nazi distinction between the human and the sub-human, the *Untermenschen,* beings who can be killed without having their death recognised as murder because they exist outside laws protecting humans, is not particular to the Nazis. This seems obvious when one considers war itself, the European witch burnings, genocidal atrocities, the suspension of human rights for refugees, various forms of lethal dehumanising racism. The expression *lebensunwertes Leben* [life unworthy of living] was coined by Karl Binding and Alfred Hoche in their influential 1920 essay 'Allowing the destruction of life unworthy of life' (Binding and Hoche 2012). Holocaust scholars have explored how eugenics provided a scientific logic for the mass extermination of human beings considered to be non-humans by the Nazi regime. The categorisation of some human beings as 'non-human' threatens all lives with the potential judgement that they do not deserve to exist. This logic, in other words, masked with the apparent objectivity of science, is capable of transforming anyone into non-humans.

Agamben also investigates Levi's understanding of the 'Mussulman', or Muslim, those human beings in the camps who were considered to be the walking dead, the 'drowned', as Levi puts it, living skeletons, non-human objects of hate and contempt by other prisoners. It is the Mussulman, argues Levi, who is the true witness of the camps. Agamben argues that an ethics that is capable of challenging the exterminatory logic of modern power must bear witness to the Mussulman. This means in effect recognising that people who are destroyed by the system are not psychologically or genetically abnormal; it is not that some people do not 'fit in' or 'survive' because they are inferior—the function of the system is the destruction of human beings. The system turns people into lives unworthy of being lived.

"Are women human?" asks Catharine A. MacKinnon (2007) in her critique of human rights laws which repeatedly erase the existence of women. Do women, those creatures historically considered to be less human than men—defective copies, spare ribs, those cows, chicks, bitches, dogs, birds, pussys, cum dumpsters, sluts, dirty whores, tarts, skanks, cunts—deserve to live? The dehumanisation of women is a central political technology in male supremacist cultures. Male supremacy is founded on the idea that women are biologically inferior to men. The girls and women who have been destroyed, driven into silence by madness, murdered or taken their own lives, are the true witnesses of male supremacy.

▽ ▽ ▽

[B]efore dying the victim must be degraded, so that the murderer will be less burdened by guilt.
—Primo Levi, *The Drowned and the Saved* (2003, p. 101)

On 10 October 2012 in Canada a 15-year-old girl named Amanda Todd hung herself after three years of relentless misogynistic online and offline persecution instigated by a paedophile stalker. Her peers repeatedly told her to commit suicide. After she died many celebrated her death. Before she died this child used flashcards to tell her story on YouTube:

Hello. I've decided to tell you about my never ending story In 7th grade I would go with friends on webcam, meet and talk to new people. Then got called stunning, beautiful, perfect etc. They wanted me to flash. So I did...Then wanted me to flash... So I did one year later...I got a msg on facebook. From him... Don't know how he knew me...It said... if you don't put on a show for me I send ur boobs. He knew my adress, school, relatives, friends family names. Christmas break...Knock at my door at 4 It was the police... my photo was sent to everyone. I then got really sick and got... Anxiety major depression panic disorder I then moved and got into Drugs + Alcohol. My anxiety got worse... couldn't go out A year past and the guy came back with my new list of friends and school. But made a facebook page. My boobs were a profile pic...Cried every night, lost all my friends and respect people had from me... again...Then nobody liked me name calling, judged...I can never get that Photo back It's out there forever... I started cutting...I promised myself never again...Didn't have any friends and I sat at lunch alone So I moved Schools again....Everything was better even though I still sat alone At lunch in the library everyday After a month later I started talking to an old guy friend We back and fourth texted and he started to say he...Liked me... Led me on He had a girlfriend Then he said come over my gf's on vacation So I did... huge mistake He hooked up with me...I thought he like me...1 week later I get a text get out of your school. His girlfriend and 15 others came including hiself... The girls and 2 others just said look around nobody likes you In front of my new School (50) people...A guy then yelled just punch her already So she did... she threw me to the ground a punched me several times Kids filmed it. I was all alone and left on the ground. I felt like a joke in this world... I thought nobody deserves this I was alone.. I like and said it was my fault and my idea. I didn't want him getting hurt, I thought he really like me but he just wanted the sex... Someone yelled punch her already. Teachers ran over but I just went and layed in a ditch and my dad found me.I wanted to die so bad... when he brought me home I drank bleach...It killed me inside and I thought I was gonna actully die. Ambulence came and brought me to the hospital and flushed me. After I got home all I saw was on facebook – She deserved it, did you wash the mud out of your hair? – I hope shes dead. nobody cared.. I moved away to another city to my moms. another school... I didn't wanna press charges because I wanted to move on 6 months has gone by... people are posting pics of bleach clorex and ditches. tagging me... I was doing alot better too. They said...She should try a different bleach. I hope she dies this time and isn't so stupid. Why do I get this? I messed up buy why follow me. They said I hope she sees this and kills herself.. Why do I get this? I messed up but why follow me. I left your guys city... Im constanty crying now.. Everyday I think why am I still here? My anxiety is horrible now. never went out this summer All from my past.. lifes never getting better.. cant go to school meet or be with people... constanly cutting. Im really depressed Im on anti depressants now and councelling and a month ago this summer I overdosed ... In hospital for 2 days..Im stuck.. whats left of me now... nothing stops I have nobody ...I need someone my name is Amanda Todd.[15]

Amanda was not trapped in her own private nightmare; she was trapped in a culture that was actively oppressing her. She had been marked as a 'life unworthy of being lived', as human waste. She was acutely aware that she was expected to kill herself. She eventually obeyed the social command to kill herself and hung herself. She was persecuted to death.

Her tragically short life highlights the eugenicist logic of misogyny, and the lethal social execution of girls (and women) who have been marked as unworthy of living merely because

---

15 Here is Amanda telling her story before she died: 'Amanda Todd's story: Struggling, bullying, suicide, self harm' <http://www.youtube.com/watch?v=ej7afkypUsc> (accessed 21 July 2013). See also an article by Naomi Wolf (2012) 'Amanda Todd suicide and social media's sexualisation of youth'. See also a transcript of Amanda's story: <http://pigletshut.blogspot.fr/2012/10/transcript-amanda-todds-story.html> (accessed 20 August 2013). Here it is noted that "as a parting gift, Best Gore has what is purported to be Amanda's autopsy photo. I won't post the link here, but it's not hard to find." Amanda is trashed in death as well as in life, her dead body flashed around the world via the world's most popular snuff website.

a single male has pointed the finger and named her as sub-human. It is tempting to think of the persecution of Amanda as an exception, yet it would be more accurate to argue that the intensity of the misogynistic hate that she was subjected to by both sexes is becoming the norm.

Amanda did not need to adjust to her oppression with therapy or antidepressants; she did not need to be further stigmatised as subnormal by being diagnosed with acute anxiety, depression or a panic disorder. Amanda needed a courageous lawyer, an advocate who could name the violation of her rights and fight for her. She needed a consciousness-raising group: a fearless grassroots feminist movement that would immediately stand shoulder to shoulder with her against those who were victimising her. She needed a *real* 'girl power movement' full of girls who have the courage to say, collectively, "enough, stand back, leave her alone, this will not be tolerated, this is political, hurt one of us and you hurt us all."

The ferocious misogyny that animates the numerous forms of oppression in the workplace, the streets, in the home, socially, politically, economically, historically, emotionally, depends on one simple but powerful strategy. The contempt and loathing women are trained to feel for each other is the single most powerful strategy misogyny has in maintaining the oppression of women. Male supremacist culture replaces the natural loving solidarity between women with hate.

In the culture of a re-loaded misogyny we are expected to be like de Sade's Juliette: competitive, sexy, and cruel towards other women. "One must, as far as possible allow the weight of one's malice to fall on those in distress; the tears drawn from misery provide a most powerful stimulant for one's nervous energies."[16] Girls and women in distress are treated with overt

---

16 Cited in Theodor W. Adorno and Max Horkheimer (1992, p. 113) in their critique of the Enlightenment. They write:

   Whereas the optimistic writers merely disavowed and denied in order to protect the indissoluble union of reason and crime, civil society and

and covert contempt because their very distress marks them as losers, pathetic weak victims.

Germaine Greer said in *The Female Eunuch*, with her usual unapologetic frankness, that women underestimate how much men hate them (1970, p. 249). However, we also underestimate how much we hate each other. And it is the hatred of each other which is perhaps even more significant than the hatred of men because, without the breaking of solidarity between women our oppression would not be possible. Internalised oppression, "the oppressors housed within them" (Freire, 1977, p. 97), viewing other women through men's eyes, false consciousness, call it what you like, woman-on-woman-contempt is the source of a profound melancholia and grief for many girls and women.

Solidarity against male domination is punished and becomes unspeakable: if you can't beat them you may as well join them and to join them is to participate in the abuse of other women, even within your own family. The oppressive necrophilic drive to conquer, divide and rule is tragically manifested in a thousand rituals of horizontal and vertical woman-on-woman oppression while the totality of male domination, the empirical historical evidence, is ignored. To paraphrase Frantz Fanon (1968), the colonised woman will first manifest this aggressiveness which has been deposited in her bones against other women.

---

domination, the dark chroniclers mercilessly declared the shocking truth. 'Heaven vouchsafes these riches to those whose hands are soiled by the murder of wives and children, by sodomy, assassination, prostitution, and atrocities; to reward me for these shameful deeds, it offers me wealth', says Clairewill when summing up her brother's life history ... In Sade as in Mandeville, private vice constitutes a predictive chronicle of the public virtues of the totalitarian era.

1.3 Room 101

> Once complete depatterning had been achieved, and the
> earlier personality had been satisfactorily wiped out, the psychic
> driving would begin. It consisted of Cameron playing his patients
> tape-recorded messages such as 'you are a good mother and
> wife and people enjoy your company'. As a behaviourist, he
> believed that if he could get his patients to absorb the messages
> on the tape, they would start behaving differently.
> With patients shocked and drugged into an almost vegetative
> state, they could do nothing but listen to the messages—for sixteen
> to twenty hours a day for weeks; in one case Cameron played a
> message continuously for 101 days.
> —Naomi Klein, *The Shock Doctrine* (2007, p. 32)

The mainstreaming of misogyny has occurred alongside
the spread of the American 'don't worry be happy' positive
thinking movement, and a radical expansion of the power of
psychiatry. 'Diagnostic creep' is a term used to describe the
ways in which everyday emotions and thoughts are being
increasingly pathologised by psychiatry. The 'mother's little
helpers' of the 1950s have been replaced by an expanding
range of psychiatric drugs designed to make women efficient,
energetic, carefree, positive consumers and sexual partners
for men. As psychiatrists are admitting, we are in the age of
the chemical makeover, and the "medicalisation of [women's]
personalities" (Kramer 1997, p. 37). To avoid being formally
or informally diagnosed as an over-sensitive 'negative psycho
bitch' one must now continually smile and project an image of
carefree positivity. Women must present themselves at all times
as beautiful, walking talking advertisements for an imperial
consumer culture.

One of the more relevant messages of Orwell's *Nineteen
Eighty-Four* is that obedience to an oppressive regime is
achieved through the control of people's emotions. Under
the Big Brother regime people are continually monitored by

each other for signs of emotional disobedience, for dissident emotions, for rebellious feelings. "I always look cheerful and I never shirk anything. Always yell with the crowd, that's what I say. It's the only way to be safe" (Orwell 1949/1981, p. 96). Inappropriate emotions, a mere twitch of a mouth, a frown, the slightest flicker of the eye at a particular moment, betray a failure to obey. "[T]o wear an improper expression on your face ... was itself a punishable offence. There was even a word for it in Newspeak: facecrime" (p. 34). Inappropriate facial expressions betray critical thinking: "Thoughtcrime does not entail death: thoughtcrime *is* death." To think against the system is to risk annihilation. One is continually observed, not just by secret cameras, but by others, for signs of betrayal to the system. Everyone is a potential informer. The deepest crime, however, the one that gives rise to all others is emotioncrime, the failure to be an *emotionally obedient* citizen.

Eventually Winston, the protagonist, is betrayed and taken to the notorious torture chamber Room 101 where he is terrorised with psychological shock and awe tactics until he betrays his fellow dissident and undergoes emotional reprogramming. The final ominous sentences of *Nineteen Eighty-Four* draw attention to the way Winston mistakes the system's conquest of himself with self-control. "But it was all right, everything was all right, the struggle was finished. He had won the victory over himself. He loved Big Brother" (p. 240). Winston has become emotionally adjusted; he is now an obedient and loving slave.

Winston comes to understand himself as the problem and not Big Brother. His experience in Room 101 'guides' him into dismissing his subversive emotions as something he needed to conquer in order to achieve happiness. He blames himself for not loving and accepting the system. Victim-blaming and self-blame have long been a hallmark of oppression.

The most pernicious victim-blaming can be found in the positive thinking self-help movement that expanded after lack of 'self-esteem' and 'confidence' were identified in sunny California some time during the 1980s as the sources of all social and political ills.

It is ironic, in the manner of a dystopian nightmare, that an advanced capitalist empire which is founded on genocide and slavery, which still functions as the global police, which has an armed population, which routinely violates international human rights, which has the largest known military industrial complex in the world, which is the world's largest producer of pornography, has also produced a saccharine ideology in which 'positive thinking' functions as a form of psychological gentrification. And it is not insignificant that the neoliberal lie that one is 110% responsible for one's life—first powerfully encapsulated by the 'alternative' conservative thinker Louise Hay, and more recently echoed by Eckhart Tolle, author of *The Power of Now* (1997/2005)—is directed at women.

Today, gendered victim-blaming has become a form of upwardly mobile common sense 'wisdom'. Now victim-blaming is expressed by voices that sound soothing, wise, calm, above all, *loving*.

It is a form of hegemonic thinking that masks misogyny with the faux compassion of spiritual wisdom. Frequently aligned with alternative lifestyle movements and 'enlightened' entrepreneurial discourses, this crypto-fascist ideology promises a New Age of global consciousness. It is hypnotically repetitive, monotonously moronic, riddled with ridiculously irrational superstitions. Most have encountered this self-empowerment neoliberal self-help discourse because it has become a form of common sense, a dominant way of explaining life.

Gloria Steinem's 1993 book *Revolution from Within* marked a turning point in the women's liberation movement, an historical moment in which the women's health movement, which had been instrumental in challenging the oppression of women through psychiatry and medicine, teamed up with the heavily psychologised self-help movement and retreated into the Self. The triumph of this 'happy thinking' is the sign of a dramatic defeatism, of a profound melancholia about social change. It is a form of extreme solipsism in which economics, politics, history, indeed material reality itself, have been replaced by a grandiose narrative about the all-powerful Self that is endowed with the magical ability to manifest a positive reality (money and so on) simply by radiating good energy.

It is also an ideology that is specifically targeted at women and promotes extreme forms of self-blame under the guise of self-empowerment, emotional maturity and responsibility. Gendered victim-blaming is today marketed as a form of self-empowerment, the foundation of physical, psychological and financial wellbeing, and as 'the secret' of a happy and abundant life. In the words of Louise Hay, author of *You Can Heal Your Life* (1984):

> WHEN WE BLAME another, we give our power away because we're placing the responsibility for our feelings on someone else.
>
> The reality of true forgiveness lies in setting ourselves free from holding on to the pain. It's simply an act of releasing ourselves from the negative energy.
>
> You're exactly what you've chosen to be in this lifetime. Of all the bodies and all the personalities that were available, you chose to be who you are—to experience this world, this lifetime, through your body, through your personality. So love your choice, for it is part of your spiritual evolution.[17]

Hay is clearly marketing self-blame to women relying on a dubious mix of flimsy ideas about psychosomatic illness (hysteria re-loaded) and the arch absurdity of the New Age conceit that one can magically manifest one's reality, and that one's private thoughts or individual emotional energies are more powerful

---

17 For tips on how to blame yourself see Louise L. Hay (2010) 'Do you give your power away?' <http://www.healyourlife.com/author-louise-l-hay/2010/01/wisdom/personal-growth/do-you-give-your-power-away> (accessed 21 July 2013).

than the global banking system, the government, the oil crisis, or interest rate rises.

Not only are we encouraged to blame ourselves for the socio-economic conditions of our lives, but she even argues that disease is a symptom of negative emotions, that polio, for example, is caused by sexual guilt. The oppressed (and even those with terminal illnesses) are merely suffering because they have 'chosen' to pollute themselves with negative emotions. Although this self-help ideology promotes itself as a form of alternative wisdom, it represents a form of extreme conservatism, a form of *emotional fascism*.

It would be a mistake to simply dismiss the New Age self-help movement as a mystification of socio-economic relations between the sexes. Women are also being instructed in how to behave, think, and feel. The self-help discourses are, in effect, instructions in sexist feminine 'feeling rules', in how to perform the obedient feminine self, in how to 'feel' feminine. Women's political power is reduced to their ability to think self-empowering thoughts such as 'I am beautiful, I love my body, I love myself' which is the intellectual equivalent of a self-inflicted lobotomy. Beneath the soporific advice to embrace the power of self-love there often lurks a snarling anti-feminism, as though feminism, and not the slings and arrows of outrageous male supremacy, were the source of women's suffering.

For example, in a chapter of the pompously titled, yet wildly successful Oprah Winfrey-sponsored *The Power of Now: A Guide to Spiritual Enlightenment*, wealthy New Age self-help spokesman for the 'Divine', Eckhart Tolle (who is claimed to be 'the most spiritually influential author in the world'), offers his celestial patriarchal opinion on "Dissolving the Collective Female Pain-Body" (p. 138). Women, he argues, have a much larger pain-body "entity" than men and this "entity" mounts monthly attacks against all women who are not "conscious". But exactly what is this "entity"?

> This consists of accumulated pain suffered by women partly through male subjugation of the female, through slavery, exploitation, rape, childbirth, child loss, and so on, over thousands of years. The emotional or physical pain that for many women precedes and coincides with the menstrual flow is the pain-body in its collective aspect that awakens from its dormancy at that time ... Let's dwell on this for a moment and see how it can become an opportunity for enlightenment (1997/2005, p. 139).

The physical reality of menstrual pain is dismissed by the time worn 'it's all in your stupid little head' strategy of the patronising patriarchal quack. It seems that Tolle (a rather diminutive middle-aged German multimillionaire with un-blinking pale blue eyes) has invented a new twist on the die-hard misogynistic insult that all women are hysterical. *Now* (as it were) hysteria is a collective "entity" born of thousands of years of female oppression. And, predictably, women are attacked by this "entity" when they menstruate. (The Greek word for 'womb' is *hystera* from which comes 'hysterical'.)

However, and this is the central idea, the ancient collective hysterical pain-body entity ectoplasm does not attack 'conscious' women every month. In fact, it seems that this 'entity' especially likes to attack *feminists* who are, of course, not 'conscious'. Ipso facto, period pain is a form of feminist hysteria and this pain ends once one's consciousness is as clean and joyfully absorbent of the *Now* as an unused sanitary napkin.

Channelling the 'Source', Tolle announces the following to women who live on planet earth:

> Apart from her personal pain-body, every woman has her share in what could be described as the collective female pain-body—unless she is fully conscious ... It is the living past in you, and if you identify with it, you identify with the past. A victim identity is the belief that the past is more powerful than the present, which is the opposite of the truth. It is the belief that other people and what they did to you are responsible for who you are now, for your emotional pain or your inability to be true to yourself (1997/2005, pp. 139–140).

Logic, it seems, is no obstacle in the pursuit of victim-bashing. Who, but goldfish, only live in the *Now*? The message, cloaked in what is presented as the benevolent authority of the Divine, is callous: 'get over it girls' ☺. If you are experiencing pain it means you are not taking responsibility for your emotions ☺. If you are in pain, it is your fault, your responsibility, because you are not 'conscious' ☺.

The injunction 'do not live in the past'—move on, let go, accept, forgive, release—is not simply about healing trauma or managing triggering. It is the kind of advice a priest might give a prisoner who has no hope of ever being released and whose only chance of happiness is managing how she relates to an environment she has no control over. Or as Orwell writes, "[h]istory has stopped. Nothing exists except an endless present in which the Party is always right" (1949/1981, p. 91).

Above all, do not identify with or act, think or feel like a feminist. Under the guise of graciously channelling a spiritual wisdom from the Divine, Tolle instructs women to cleanse themselves of political consciousness in the name of becoming "conscious:"

> Some women who are already conscious enough to have relinquished their victim identity on the personal level are still holding on to a collective victim identity:'what men did to women'.They are right— and they are also wrong.They are right inasmuch as the collective female pain-body is in large part due to male violence inflicted on women ... They are wrong if they derive a sense of self from this fact and thereby keep themselves imprisoned in a collective victim identity. If a woman is still holding on to anger, resentment, or condemnation, she is holding on to her pain-body.This may give her a comforting sense of identity, of solidarity with other women, but it is keeping her in bondage to the past and blocking full access to her essence and true power ... So do not use the pain-body to give you an identity. Use it for enlightenment instead.Transmute it into consciousness. One of the best times for this is during menses (1997/2005, p. 141).

On one level Tolle's suggestion that women achieve enlightenment by cleansing themselves of a collective political awareness of women's oppression in some kind of psychic menstrual hut is so absurd it is funny. But given that Tolle is regarded as the world's most influential spiritual author it is important to uncover the layers of misogynistic thinking operating here.

The popularity of this kind of thinking is not due to any originality on the author's part. Tolle's books are a pastiche of self-help and New Age clichés. Self-help books such as these resonate with and support the imperial politics of United States neo-liberalism, of a highly militarised patriarchal capitalism that requires docile, happy and obedient female consumers who don't march, strike and protest, leave husbands or join unions. In an era in which women's working lives are increasingly precarious, where under-employment, part-time and casual contracts in the secondary labour market are a reality for the majority of women, where so many women live with the perpetual threat of poverty and social exclusion, women cannot afford to fall apart, to grieve, suffer, to fail to obey the male supremacist 'feeling rules' of performing oneself as perpetually happy. The old saying 'smile and the world smiles with you, cry and you cry alone' is a warning for women, the *smiling class*. The emotional labour of the *Now* is similar to the effort required in the service economy to be continually other-focused and happy, nice and obedient to the demands of customers, employers, and so forth. One must not think if thinking produces a frown or perhaps a less than happy sounding voice. *Do not commit emotioncrime.* Smile while you clean the toilet with heavy-duty chemicals that make your eyes smart, try not to inhale, and scrub away joyfully with a sense of appreciation for your life.

Women are bullied into thinking that a man's word is correct, to deny their own reality, to doubt their own senses, to second-guess and doubt themselves continually, to erase their own knowledge, to disavow their own experiences. They are taught not to inhabit the lived reality of their own bodies; they are sexually, physically and emotionally abused out of their minds and bodies. The culture of male supremacy subjects women to continual 'gaslighting', to a perpetual crazy-making disavowal of their material and emotional realities.[18] How perfect then that women are instructed to inhabit a *Now* which contains only the prescribed permissible feminine emotions of joy, bliss and happiness, which is all about 'acceptance' (also known as 'obedience') which is based on a radical historical amnesia.

New Age self-help advice can be read as instructions for women about how to adapt to their own exploitation, how to become more efficient and obedient wage slaves in an exploitative economy in which they face unemployment and under-employment, where they have very little control of their lives. It is advice for the female 'precariat', the majority of women who have long lost security at any level.[19] Patriarchal capitalism requires female wage slaves who radiate approval for their own exploitation, who smile continuously, who rapidly move on from one exploitative situation to another without blaming anyone but themselves, who can appear to rise above the numerous socio-economic and sexual threats to a life made viciously precarious.

One must *Smile or Die*, as the title of Barbara Ehrenreich's 2009 book on how breast cancer is framed as the outcome of women's negative emotions, puts it. These feminine 'feeling rules' are so controlling that a frown or any sign of negative or

---

18 Taken from the plot of the 1938 Patrick Hamilton play, *Gas Light*. 'Gaslighting' is a form of mental abuse in which false information is presented with the intent of making a victim doubt his or her own memory, perception and sanity by denying the abuse ever occurred, or trying to disorientate, and therefore discredit, the abused.

19 For an early discussion of women as the precariat class see Maria Mies (1982/2012).

revolutionary or dissident emotion can lead to social rejection. Many women are told to smile more at work. The seemingly light-hearted suggestion conceals a threat: 'smile or we will persecute you'. Women must appear to be happy and positive, not because they are, but because to be otherwise is to risk political persecution. After all, women have always been smiling advertisements for toilet cleaning products, cars, fast food, watches, smart phones, make-up, the entire debris of patriarchal capitalism and so surely they must smile in real life because above all they must perform themselves as advertisements for the endless fun and games of male supremacy.

The rhetoric of this form of pop-psychology has also been adopted by those who aspire to social mobility, for beneath the mannered exotic serenity of the beautifully responsible ones, there lies a rather less exalted motive for purchasing the rhetoric of 'responsibility'. Quite simply, it provides one with a refined and sanctimonious pop-psych approved 'noble' form of a kind of victim-blaming which makes the traditional right-wing contempt for those who have failed the barbaric social Darwinism survival of the fittest test seem almost, but not quite, benevolent.

The Oprah Winfrey-sponsored book *The Secret* (2006), for example—written by Rhonda Byrne and influenced by Wallace Wattles' 1910 book *The Science of Getting Rich*—has sold over 19 million copies. The premise is that if you think good things, good things will happen to you and if you think bad things, bad things will happen to you. This 'idea', if one might call it that, is argued to be an ancient secret known only to exotic cultures, the 'illuminati', elite bands of geniuses and the rich and powerful. *The Secret* is a gift, the gift of unlimited power, joy, bliss, money, love, beauty, flat TV screens and stomachs, expensive cars and apartments. Feel good, visualise good, think good, be good and good things will 'manifest' in your life. In other words, if you are oppressed in any way (and the discourse has no room to acknowledge the politics of oppression) then it is your own fault and you must therefore cleanse yourself of negative thinking.

Have you been diagnosed with breast cancer? Were you sacked during the GFC? Let's think about how you chose to attract this into your life with your negative energy.

At the end of the documentary *The Secret* (2006) a middle-aged white woman sits on a beach gazing peacefully at a sunset while a soothing loving male voice-over says, "this is for you, mother." In a twist worthy of Orwell, the book and the film market self-empowerment and the secret to abundance, wealth, love and all the wonderful things on offer under patriarchal capitalism as *self-blame*. Self-blame is for you, mother.

In effect, blaming women for their own suffering is marketed as an innovative yet ancient cosmic insight, the secret to becoming 'conscious'. Self-blame becomes the spiritual evolution of the Self. Blaming other women is transformed into a generously loving act, an act of wisdom and friendship, a sharing of enlightened consciousness.

This 'empowering' cult of victim-blaming cuts women's political consciousness off at the knees. Feminist consciousness is implicitly framed as déclassé, a sign that one is not 'conscious' or spiritually evolved, that one belongs to an emotionally inferior class of women, that one is not 'feminine'. In order to evolve one's consciousness (and succeed in love and work) one must not only distance oneself from feminism, but also secure one's status within the evolved group by diagnosing the suffering of women you know as an individual failure to take responsibility for their lives. The goal is a mass cleansing of the female mind of all revolutionary thought, of critical thinking, above all of a feminist consciousness which does not forget, which does not forgive, which seeks collective justice.

Tolle preaches, in effect, a misogynistic, anti-feminist quietism. The depoliticisation of the *Now* which is meant to occur continually, is the depoliticisation of an entire woman's life. She is torn from her historical context, such that all 'her problems' are read as an attachment to 'the past', and suffering (or negative thinking) of any kind is seen as a symptom of a failure to become conscious and be responsible for one's life. The insult should not be underestimated.

2.0 The New Ageism: Emotional Engineering

Much has been written about the intensified pressure to look young. The trillion-dollar imperial propaganda machine, which combines the fashion, diet, cosmetic, entertainment and cosmetic surgery industries, subjects women to relentless psychological harassment. These industries herd women into obeying the commands of the new ageism by proliferating the rarely contested warnings about the uselessness, the sexual and social redundancy, of older women. One must appear youthful, or one is destined for the trash heap, thrown out with the rest of the women who have exceeded their shelf life, their synthetic patriarchal use-by date. Women's lives are under intimate political attack by ageism. This is not an existential dread of non-existence, but rather the political dread of deadly social exclusion and contempt, poverty, lack of job security, housing, and increased exposure to the woman-hating fury of patriarchal imperialism that has been unleashed during their Global Financial Crisis.

Ageism is the intimate colonisation of embodied time by the vampiric forces of patriarchal capitalism that installs an ideological time-bomb in the female mind that ticks with the incessant and cruel warning that the passing of time is something for which women must be punished. Women, far more than men, are judged by how old they are and how old they look. The threatening ticking of male domination reduces women's social and economic worth to how 'fresh' we appear.

The jubilantly vacuous self-empowered ever bubbly and frantically energetic nymphette is the new ideal. And it is no coincidence that the escalating political assault of ageism has coincided with the unprecedented commercial sexualisation of girl children. Critics of the sexualisation of girls are often shouted down for being boring killjoys who are merely envious of younger girls, who are, in a word, 'old'. Ironically, many who defend the sexualisation of girls are themselves several generations older than teenagers. In a desperate bid to demonstrate that they are young at heart, postmodern hipsters, the corporate apologist neo-liberal intellectual celebrity mafia find themselves in alliance with the new ageism when they overtly or covertly mock critics of the sexualisation of girls for being old (mothers, old-school feminists, wowser parents, uncool uptight old moral panic fogey types, etc.).

The idea that females are best when fresh, and have a shelf life like a packet of digestive biscuits, is still entrenched. That women must be consumed by a man while they still look young is central to the new ageism which seems to be geared to making older single women feel like an apologetic waste of space merely because they are alive past the age of 25.[20] "What is the use of a woman over 25?" sneers our gloriously enlightened democracy. In March 2013 so-called communist China announced that unmarried women over the age of 27 are "leftover women" (Fincher, 2012). This is how the shift from communism to capitalism is marketed.

While the new ageism is clearly an important tool of oppression in the emerging social fascism of shiny hypermarket misogyny, little has been written about how it is re-shaping personality. Not only are women under increasing pressure to conform to the multiple demands that they look youthful (in a

---

20 See, for example, <http://laidnyc.wordpress.com/2013/08/05/dont-marry-any-woman-older-than-25/> (accessed 14 August 2013).

polished, upwardly mobile way), but now one must *act* youthful as well. Frown lines between the brows are one of the most heavily-targeted areas for Botox treatment, but the ideological force of erasing frown lines which have been gained by fighting for survival in a woman-hating culture goes beyond the needle in the head. Now the *internal* frown must be smoothed away to make way for a carefree, youthful personality. Stress, as we are told endlessly, is so ageing, a sign that one is slipping downwards, expiring one's use, and becoming a burden to others. One must have a youthful, fun-loving, energetic, perpetually optimistic, carefree, girlish personality. Ageism has become intensely psychological, a way of policing the emotional lives of women, and therefore, the way they are permitted to name and fight their oppression.

Writing about dominant post-feminist femininity, Rosalind Gill argues that

> [w]hat marks out the present moment as distinctive, however, are three features: first, the dramatically increased intensity of self-surveillance, indicating the intensity of the regulation of women (alongside the disavowal of such regulations); secondly, the extensiveness of surveillance over entirely new spheres of life and intimate conduct; and thirdly, the focus upon the psychological—upon the requirements to transform oneself and remodel one's interior life. For instance, being 'confident', 'carefree' and 'unconcerned about one's appearance' are now central aspects of femininity in their own right—even as they sit alongside injunctions to meet standards of beauty that 'only a mannequin could achieve' (Kilbourne, 1999 cited in Gill, 2008, p. 440).

Rosalind Gill quite rightly points out that the 'makeover paradigm'—which she identifies as intensely ageist—and the psychological reinvention of the self as 'carefree' is not only heavily implicated in the marketing of liberal feminism as a youth movement, but in a compulsory youthful personality that is characterised by a lack of concern about oppression.

Adult women, with adult concerns, it seems, are sexually undesirable. One U.S website encapsulates what Florence Rush noted in *The Best Kept Secret* (1980): nymphettes are desirable. For example, the following insights about men are offered under the heading: 'What men find irresistible Secret #2: Lead with your "youthfulness"':

> A man desires youthfulness in a woman he would consider spending all his time with. Youthfulness means a state of being innocent and childlike, and this is something that stimulates men on a subconscious level to crave. Youth is an attitude. Most women are very burned out inside from the obligations of the world, and this has a very strong effect on how men will perceive you ... Men sense when a woman is fresh and has kept herself separate from the negativity of others' opinions and when a woman has allowed herself to be burned out, burdened with obligations and has lost touch with the little girl within. A child playing on a playground hasn't been burdened by the world's "adulthood" and "responsibilities" yet. All she cares about is PLAYING ... in the sand, swinging on the swings and having fun. She is fresh; she doesn't hold onto the past and isn't worried about the future ... It's just a matter of learning what type of energy men are emotionally attracted to in a woman.[21]

The advice given to women here is symptomatic of the ways in which women are now under pressure to pretend they are positive, playful girls in order to attract adult men. It is tempting to call the new ageism a form of affective paedophilia if the preferred feminine personality mimics a playful little girl. Reverse the gender and it becomes clear: men are not expected to behave like little boys playing in sandpits in order to attract sexual partners. But once in relationships, many grown men oddly start acting like teenagers and position their partners as mothers/caretakers, as Betty McLellan recognised in *Help! I'm Living with a ~~Man~~ Boy* (1995).

---

21 See the startling website: <http://www.yintegrity.com/blog/12-thing-a-woman-does-that-men-find-irresistible> (accessed 21 July 2013).

Articles such as 'Most important things men find attractive in women' by Marisa Swanson[22] yet again emphasise the importance of being childishly playful."

> Many men list this in their top priorities when they're talking girlfriend or wife material. A girl who doesn't take herself or life too seriously is a big asset, as many women tend to complain or get upset about things that men view as trivial. Learn to laugh at the unfair or unsavoury parts of life and you will go far with your man. Men also like women who are playful, regardless of their age. Being 'youthful' in spirit is very attractive to men and goes hand in hand with a good sense of humor.

Smile, laugh, don't take yourself too seriously because men think your problems are trivial anyway, and entertain your potential big daddy master with your girlish playfulness. Cultivate a LOL approach to your suffering. Laugh at yourself and male domination laughs with you. Cry and you will be rejected. Be a happy little girl and don't complain about being oppressed. "The more innocent, smiley, girly and child-like you are, the more happiness you are likely to bring to a man."[23]

Not only are women advised to seduce men by pretending to be playful little girls but they are also told to practise having a girlish voice, slightly high-pitched and lilting, to giggle and even, according to a 2010 study published in the *Journal of Evolutionary Psychology*, to make sure that their heads are "tilted slightly downward." Because apparently "tilting her face upward made the woman appear more masculine, and therefore less attractive to the men in the study" conducted by the University of Newcastle (*The Telegraph*, 23 November 2010).

---

22 <http://www.ehow.com/list_7483281_important-things-men-attractive-women.html#page=1> (accessed 21 July 2013).
23 <http://www.whatdomenreallythink.com/howto/tips-on-becoming-a-feminine-woman.php> (accessed 21 July 2013).

If the compulsory rejuvenation of the female body is a key feature of the new ageism, so too is the rejuvenation of the female personality. The desirable feminine type is girlish, light, playful, and as threatening as a Disney cartoon. As a woman writes in the popular American 'The art of being a feminine woman' blog in the section '7 tips on how to attract a man who wants to marry you':

> [M]y husband used to say that if you sliced me open, a beautiful cloud of Disney characters would fly forth—Bambi, Thumper, Winnie the Pooh, Snow White, Cinderella, Dumbo, The Fairy Godmother, Alice, all those singing bluebirds that dressed the princesses.[24]

Like a pink papier mâché piñata, once cut open, the beautiful girl-woman pours forth a sweet, chirping, bubbly menagerie of happy cartoons. There are no 'dark' and 'wild' negative feelings here, only the 'light' tamed emotions of a sunny Disneyland. No need for a Stepford-wife-style lobotomy, something else has occurred.

2.1 Girl Power: Woman, You Gotta Be a Girl-Child Now!

Imagine an adult liberation movement that called itself 'boy power'. Or imagine that a diverse and complex, historically powerful global liberation movement which was combating the violent socio-economic and sexual oppression of a people had become known as 'girl power'. Imagine a political platform for socio-economic revolution that was encapsulated in sound bites such as 'we are all beautiful no matter what we look like' or 'self-empowerment is self-confidence'. In a brief article 'Do you feel any more confident yet?' (2012) Germaine Greer observes that a certain patronising proselytising about

---

24 <http://theseductivewoman.blogspot.fr/p/all-articles.html> (accessed 21 July 2013).

the importance of being seen as beautiful suffuses mainstream feminism.

> At an event in Amsterdam recently, I was ordered by a woman on the stage to take the hand of the woman next to me, who happened to be the 76-year-old Hedy d'Ancona, and tell her that she was beautiful. This was more conducive to her self-esteem, apparently, than reminding her that, having served as a minister under two Dutch governments, as a member of the European Parliament, and as chairman of Dutch Oxfam, she was immensely distinguished and I was honoured to be sitting next to her.

In other words, self-esteem is equated with being recognised as beautiful. The vacuous equation contains a cutting insult: narcissism is more important to women than human rights. It is highly unlikely that male political elders are asked to hold each other's hands and tell each other they are handsome.

In 2001 the *Oxford English Dictionary* defined 'girl power' as "power exercised by girls; spec. a self-reliant attitude among girls and young women."[25] The *Cambridge Dictionary* offers the following definition: "[T]he idea that women and girls should be confident, make decisions, and achieve things independently of men, or the social and political movement based on this idea."[26] This definition of girl power subtly encapsulates the popular transformation of the women's liberation movement into a heavily psychologised, consumer-friendly, self-esteem movement. Feminism is implicitly reduced to an "idea" that girls and women should be confident, make decisions, and achieve "things" without male assistance.

Embedded in this reduction is the lie of "enlightened sexism" (Douglas, 2010) which masks escalating sexual inequality

---

25 *Oxford English Dictionary* cited in PR Newswire <http://www.prnewswire.co.uk/news-releases/girl-power-enters-the-oxford-english-dictionary-155487565.html> (accessed 21 July 2013).

26 *Cambridge Dictionary Online* <http://dictionary.cambridge.org/dictionary/british/girl-power> (accessed 21 July 2013).

with the cheap trick that feminism has achieved equality for women, and now all we need is enough confidence to take advantage of the abundant opportunities offered by a benevolent woman-friendly culture. The self-empowerment narratives that came out of the Girl Power Movement were heavily attached to girlhood: self-esteem was tagged with girl, smuggling in larger ideas about how women should behave, feel and think by repackaging feminism as something that is girlish. As a ruling idea, the girlie power ideal also transmits ruling class femininity. There are no 'pramface', 'mingers', 'pigs', over-weight, cheaply dressed, depressed, struggling, young single mothers from public housing estates, exploited or unemployed lower-class 'chav' girls interrupting the Paris Hilton power-posturing of the new pink empowerment. Sorry, no victims allowed.

"Today is International Women's Day," announced a 2011 Australian article,

> ... a day of celebrating the achievements of women-folk around the world. We've made a list of ten Australian ladies whose achievements and talent are an inspiration to their peers, and prove that Girl Power is much more than just a popular Nineties' catchphrase.[27]

The women who are celebrated here are not revolutionary working-class feminists; some are supermodels. All of which is a far cry from communist Clara Zetkin's vision of International Women's Day in 1910.[28] However, the article is correct in saying that "Girl Power is much more than just a popular Nineties' catchphrase." The ageism that is embedded in girl power has infantilised mainstream feminism but also turned its back on the 'old-school feminism' of the past for being too wrinkly

---

27 'Girl Power: Ten inspiring and influential Australian women' <http://www. pedestrian.tv/arts-andculture/features/girl-power-ten-inspiring-and-influential-australia/37787.htm> (accessed 13 March 2011).

28 See <http://www.internationalwomensday.com/about.asp#.UgcvxFP98Vc> for a brief history of International Women's Day.

to be invited to the party. If the sexualisation of children carries with it the hidden demand that adult women look like pampered prepubescents, girl power childifies feminism into yet another kidult commodity for the upwardly mobile.

Beginning in the mid-1990s, the Girl Power Movement was always a mainstream pop culture phenomenon that was about as threatening to patriarchy as a lacy push-up bra, and as welcome to "cool capitalism" (McGuigan, 2009) as is any new enormous mass market. The cynical Spice Girls appropriation of feminist rhetoric claimed Baby Spice as a 'freedom fighter' and ordained Margaret Thatcher 'the milk snatcher' as an honorary Spice Girl. Today, girl power has become synonymous with glamorous, skinny young action girls with designer haircuts who somehow beat up gangs of large muscular male thugs without being sexually assaulted. Or with films and sitcoms about young upper-middle-class 'kick-ass' professionals who strut through life in obscenely expensive clothes. Or with attractive young middle-class white girls flashing their breasts in protests about sexual violence. Or with acne cream. But shaking one's breasts and ass, preening in designer clothes, or dabbing acne cream onto pimples, has never been a very useful political strategy for overthrowing power. As McRobbie argues, the new girlie consumer-friendly neoconservative feminism is

> ill-equipped to deal with war, with militarism, with 'resurgent patriarchy' with questions of cultural difference, with race and ethnicity and notably with the instrumentalisation of feminism on the global political stage (2009, p. 158).

Many 'killjoys' (or whatever the current equivalent term is for those who are disgusted by imperialist propaganda) have argued that the 'movement' is politically regressive and is a not-so-subtle backlash against feminism. The colour of the backlash is a nice girly pink. But the off-colour reality is that the vast majority of women are being emotionally and physically crushed in demeaning low-paid part-time or casual jobs in the secondary labour market with the added pressure to now mask the brutal impact of prolonged economic exploitation on their bodies and minds with the command to spend their hard-earned money on looking youthfully fresh. And thanks to the shrieking-throw-your-hands-up-in-the-air-and-spin-around-in-your-stilettos-giggling-duck-mouthed-selfie-group-hug of girl power, adult women are now expected to mask the lived experience of incessant and aggressive exploitation with the fresh, girly, sexed-up confidence of a euphoric millionaire about to storm Harrods with her American Express card.

On 21 July 2013 a popular feminist Facebook Inc. group, 'a girl's guide to taking over the world', posted the *Revolutionary Lives Manifesto*. It reads:

> The world needs revolutionaries, the world needs people like you. Revolutionaries challenge people, society and the world to ensure a better future. They share their brilliance, vision, kindness, LOVE, leadership, creativity and gratitude. They question what really makes them happy and healthy. BEING REVOLUTIONARY MEANS: Leading with integrity and without a title, Following happiness, Cherishing life's wisdom, appreciating life's joys, CULTIVATING MASTERY. Being MINDFUL, being PLAYFUL, being PERSISTENT, CHOOSING THE PATHWAY ONLY YOU CAN SEE. Following your bliss and inspiration. Pursuing a purpose bigger than oneself. Nurturing optimism and wellbeing. THIS IS THE PRACTICE OF A REVOLUTIONARY.[29]

In short, being a feminist revolutionary means conforming to dominant scripts about being a happy, healthy, playful, enterprising, self-improving MIDDLE-CLASS girl.

The framing of the confident uppity nymphette as the 'It' girl of the post-feminist Girl Power Movement depends on an ageist revulsion for the serious political maturity of feminism. 'Old-school feminism', which is all too frequently collapsed

---

29 <http://revolutionarylives.com/blog/2011/11/30/revolutionary-lives-manifesto.html> (accessed 15 August 2013).

with feminism itself, is dismissed by the anti-adultism of post-feminism as the baggage of an embarrassingly unattractive past full of miserable crazy old cows who frowned a lot and didn't know how to have a good time and obviously suffered from low self-esteem and victim-mentality problems—or something like that. Offering a critique of third wave/third way feminist discourses, McRobbie writes:

> The barrier to individuality, and individual expression was no longer 'the patriarchy' but feminism (Baumgardner and Richards, 2004, p. 65). This is an anti-feminist argument, casting elders as implicitly unattractive and embittered ... There is a refrain repeated which is that 'girl is good' and that feminism should not mean having to abandon that terrain of enjoyable activities such as 'knitting and canning vegetables or decorating' (2009, pp. 157–158).

It is also an ageist argument brimming with a disavowed fear of exceeding one's patriarchal use-by date without 'making it' in patriarchal capitalism.

The main prize is access to patriarchal wealth—not revolutionary social change: feminism is framed as a symbolic 'cock block' that reduces girls' chances of upward social mobility. Ageism is mobilised in an opportunistic contempt for feminism in the hope that conforming to the new girly normative femininity will be rewarded by greater access to the patriarchal pie. The Mills & Boon dream of marrying a wealthy man and living 'happily ever after' is more dominant that ever. Submission to sadistic alpha-male bores is eroticised in best sellers such as *Fifty Shades of Grey* (James, 2012) where Christian Grey silently thumps about like a clumsy version of the wealthy sexual tyrants in Anne Desclos' *The Story of O* (1954/2013). Clever girls, it is often said, know how to attract Mr Right, and Mr Right, as Madonna sang in 'Material Girl' (1984)[30] is always the one with the cold hard cash.

---

30 <http://en.wikipedia.org/wiki/Material_Girl> (21 July 2013).

It is not insignificant that the image of the pouting, self-empowered 'It' girl, gyrating through thousands of advertisements, films, songs and sitcoms emerged during a time when global neo-liberalism began intensifying the socio-economic attack on women and children's lives. In the United States in 1996, the federal Aid to Families with Dependent Children program was destroyed and replaced by the Personal Responsibility and Work Opportunity Reconciliation Act, which Bill Clinton proudly declared would "end welfare as we know it."[31] Those most harmed were single mothers. The sociologist Loïc Wacquant, echoing what many socialist feminists argued, describes the neo-liberal attacks as the "(re)masculinisation of the state" (2009, p. 15). Third way 'Cool Britannia' rapidly followed the United States' neo-liberal 'empowerment' model in the 1990s, and Australia also began its slow-but-steady attack on women, especially mothers, who needed financial support to survive in a society which had been inflicted on them since birth.

Girl power embodies one of the key tenets of neo-liberalism, "the cultural trope of individual responsibility" (Wacquant, 2009, pp. 306–307). Beneath the saccharine, airbrushed girls-can-do-anything image is a ruthless contempt for women and girls who have not sold themselves to the right bidder by performing the neo-liberal striptease of self-empowerment. Being smart about men doesn't mean being smart about the urgent need for revolutionary change, it means playing the game so that one can attract a good earner. Behind the new ageist opportunism lurks a desperate attempt at pragmatism born of the recognition that the social safety nets protecting single women are being shredded by neo-liberalism. But it is a desperate gamble based on a radical over-estimation of the power that youthful female sexuality has over men, and

---

31 'Welfare reform press statement' Bill Clinton Press Conference <http://www.youtube.com/watch?v=J6QOuoqeOFQ> (accessed 14 August 2013). See also Clinton (22 August 2006).

a radical under-estimation of the growing forces of misogyny. The image of carefree, positive-individualism amounts to a 'Pick me! Pick me!' plea. Aware of her competition, she learns that she must out-smile other girls, and contort herself into ever more painful denials of her lived reality by performing herself as youthfully confident.

Feminism is seen as obsolete precisely because it has been stigmatised as a social movement driven by old women, who are vilified by patriarchy for being unattractive hags who fail to take responsibility for their lives. In an ideological perversion worthy of George Orwell's *Nineteen Eighty-Four*, neo-liberal social fascism reframes feminism as a discourse of irresponsibility and disempowerment. The generational splitting within third wave feminism can be understood as a symptom of the growing dominance of a new form of misogynistic ageism. The postmodern idealisation of subversive desire is often little more than an intellectually gentrified form of neo-liberal individualism. Not so subtly, the new ageism separates political positions within feminism along the lines of the traditional and the cool, such that forms of oppression identified by second wave feminism are shunned as belonging to an obsolete political tradition that is hopelessly out of touch with the complexities of contemporary life. At its best, the ageism that feeds the political disconnect between the 'old' history of revolutionary feminist activism and theory and 'youthful' third way feminism hides the deepening wounds of economic violence by 'coolfarming' new subversive practices from the underclass in order to applaud the resilient dignity of oppressed youth.[32]

But the continual re-freshing of identity politics does little to stop the re-loading of the new world order. The symbolic

---

32 See Gloor (2010) on 'coolfarming'. Spying on the underclass in order to see what radical youth might be into in order to appropriate and exploit it is a by now venerable marketing practice which is strangely mirrored in cultural studies and the cultural industries within the academy.

and actual violence of neo-liberalism, the brutal contempt for the majority who cannot afford to embrace the promised liberation of creative self-transformation because they are being slowly or rapidly shoved into the gutter, is tragically intensified by a third way neo-feminist disavowal of the deepening misogyny of economic oppression.

Writing about the explosion of neo-liberalism in the 1990s in America, Thomas Frank observes that "'destroying the old' and making the world safe for billionaires has been as much a cultural and a political operation as an economic one" (Frank, 2001, p. 15). Billionaire-friendly feminism, for example, attempts to destroy 'old-school feminist' critiques of women's sexual exploitation in order to support the sex industry. It mystifies economic oppression with appeals to the consumer sovereignty of young prostitutes and young women who buy into sex-industry-built identities and practices, and it supports deregulated corporate oppression with anti-government hipster rhetoric. The new conservatism masks a support for authoritarian capitalism with the rhetoric of transgression.

> Enthusiasm for the new high-tech economy, the Internet, and so on, brought together right-wing libertarians and left-wing academics. Management ideology with its 'revolutionary' rhetoric had cultivated a populist legitimacy for free-market capitalism. It now associated business with popular culture in opposition to any kind of elitism (McGuigan, 2009, p. 137).

Significantly, accusing 'old' feminist critiques of the sex industry of political elitism is a common tactic of billionaire-friendly feminism. If, as Thatcher once said, "[e]conomics is the method but the object is to change the soul" (Harvey, 2005) then the 'soul' or emotional life of women is being grown down by the promise that neo-liberalism rewards youthfully tolerant libertarian femininity.[33] 'Old–school feminism' is so intolerant, so grumpy and boring.

In order to cling to the precarious social status of youthfulness, women today are coerced into assuming the attitude of a girl who has stuck her finger up at the older generation of feminists (Bray, 2011, pp. 118–121). Identifying with feminism in any small way, by voicing the barest hint of a critique of men, is to risk being seen as ugly, old, and very possibly, mentally ill.[34] Suddenly, it is as though one has been diagnosed with a personality disorder, aged ten years and put on weight. Oddly, criticising patriarchy makes your bum look big in the eyes of some.

2.2 The Inner Girl-Child Liberation Front

Before girl power giggled into popular consciousness as the fresh new face of sexy (non)feminism, there was another girly movement posing as feminism. The Inner Child Movement (helped along by Gloria Steinem's 1993 *Revolution from Within*) taught adult victims of male violence that recovery required regressing into a girl–child. Drawing, painting, working with photos, group regressions, teddy hugging, eating fattening foods, hitting pillows, playing like a child, dialoguing with an imaginary child, writing letters to her or drawing pictures of her, and generally acting out the Wounded Inner Child in order to release repressed girlish playfulness, was more important than joining a union, taking a perpetrator to court, or other grown-up things. In the words of John Bradshaw, a leader in the Inner Child Movement, healing involves the "right to offer no reasons or excuses for justifying your behaviour, the right to say 'I don't care'" (1992, pp. 161–162). Like, *whatever*! If women have been historically ridiculed for being childish and not as emotionally and mentally evolved as men, here came a

---

33 See Harvey (2005) for a history of neoliberalism.

34 See, for example, McDonough (2013) 'I'm not a feminist, but …'

movement that framed immaturity as a redemptive feminine quality.

In one popular 1990 Inner Child self-help book called *Rescuing the 'Inner Child': Therapy for Adults Sexually Abused as Children* by therapist Penny Parks, women's political knowledge and energetic anger is herded into domestic psycho-dramas with teddy bears and pillows:

> While hitting the pillow, the victim should say emphatically (a loud whisper will do if others are in the house) such things as,'*I hate you!*', or '*No!*' ... [I]f washing windows, they can picture the problem person's face under the vigorous rub of their cloth ... Releasing anger from the 'child' state will begin to free the victim from depression, temper tantrums and self-sabotage (1990, pp. 108–109).

As for justice:

> [I]f the abuser is still alive and perhaps living down the street and if you are left with a raging anger, try the pillow bashing exercise you will learn about later in this book ... to let off steam (1990, p. 15).

Instead of seeking justice, the victim is instructed to draw pictures in which her adult self rescues her wounded Inner Child from the clutches of her rapist. This is infantilising and humiliating virtual justice: the criminal justice system is replaced with hitting pillows and private drawings.

In 1992 Gloria Steinem, former head of one of the most powerful feminist organisations in the world—the American National Organization for Women—and editor of the influential feminist magazine *Ms*, dedicated her international best seller *Revolution from Within: A Book of Self-Esteem* to

> women, men, children, and even *nations*—whose power has been limited by a lack of self-esteem. It is dedicated to anyone who respects the unique self inside a child, and inspired by women whose self-esteem is making the deepest *revolution*.

Self-esteem, yes, but for whom, and to do what? "Each of us has an inner child of the past who lives within us" (p. 38), instructs Steinem. Self-esteem, she declares, is "the basis of any real democracy" (p. 10), and a "prerequisite for democracy" (p. 12), because, apparently, low self-esteem is the psychic origin of all forms of destructive behaviour from child abuse in the home to mass totalitarian violence. She argues that "one of the crucial differences between the despot and the creative leader is low self-esteem versus high self-esteem" (pp. 16–17). The astonishing confidence of oppressive tyrants seems to be strangely overlooked.

It is the Inner Girl-Child, not the collective organising of feminist revolutionaries, which now promises liberation from male domination and an end to the oppression of women. The desire for political change is diagnosed as a simple longing for self-esteem, and a desire to recover the redemptive plenitude promised by the happy girly Inner Child. The Inner Child represents the True Self, the Inner Voice, feelings, the Universal I which, writes Steinem, "preceded patriarchy, racism, class systems, and other hierarchies that ration self-esteem" (p. 32). The subject of these combative hierarchical worlds is diagnosed as the false low self-esteem self, the toxic, damaged, and self-destructive product of abusive adult power relations. The healthy Inner Girl-Child of feminism is happy, spontaneous, confident. A bit like Shirley Temple perhaps, singing and tap-dancing with an assortment of talking animals and large Disney butterflies, having huffed and puffed at pillows, and done lots and lots of drawings in crayon in order to purge herself of any bad feelings she might hold about having been raped.

Under a subheading in the first chapter, "Self-Esteem Is Personal: An Inner Child of the Past" Steinem publically self-diagnoses her two decades of feminist activism as the acting out of her wounded inner child. Just as she had cared for her mentally ill, demanding and neglectful mother as a child, she then acted out "a parallel kind of caretaking for a magazine and a movement" (p. 35) as an adult. The time had come, implied Steinem, to leave behind those needy old women. Wooohooo! All girls really want to do with their lives is have fun, fun, fun, sings Cyndi Lauper as she skips around wobbling her head about. Both the Inner Child Movement and the Girl Power Movement promote a particular kind of girl. She is happy, pert, playful and revolutionary in an endearing poke-your-tongue-out and flash-your-knickers kind of way, she likes pretty things, chocolate, and small fluffy animals. She smiles and giggles a lot. She is always positively self-empowered because she has high self-esteem, and she can do, and have, anything she wants.

The perverse ageist disconnect between the command to look, think and feel like a confident perpetually enthusiastic fun loving girl-child with the whole world at her pink, varnished toenails, and the lived realities of girls' and women's increasingly harsh oppression, is a key feature of the new misogyny. The new *affective ageism* is a form of emotional work which takes a heavy toll on women's lives and which contributes to the reproduction of women's oppression today. Ageism has become a form of emotional control, strongly aligned with the positive-thinking movement that emerged within the military empire that is the United States. Not only are women punished for failing to look like teenagers, but they are also punished for failing to present themselves as youthfully positive no matter what their lives are like. As Barbara Ehrenreich observes:

> What has changed, in the last few years, is that the advice to at least act in a positive way has taken on a harsher edge. The penalty for non-conformity is going up, from the possibility of job loss and failure to social shunning and complete isolation (2009, p. 55).

The gender of the positive thinking movement has often been identified as feminine. Women have long been the smiling class. Fail to smile and one is often reminded to, sometimes by bellowing male strangers in the street: 'Give us a smile, luv!' Now, however, the imperative to act positive has joined forces with ageism: youthful enthusiasm and a fresh, upbeat approach have become synonymous with healthy self-esteem. Negativity of any kind is not only pathologised as 'toxic' but is read as a sign that one is burnt-out, past it, emotionally 'over the hill'. Positive thinking is rejuvenating. Being positive is collapsed with having a youthful attitude. To recall the dating advice of a United States website,

> men sense when a woman is fresh and has kept herself separate from the negativity of others' opinions and when a woman has allowed herself to be burned out, burdened with obligations and has lost touch with the little girl within.[35]

In the savagely cruel parlance of neo-liberalism, being burnt-out is framed as a choice, and nothing to do with chronic exploitation and abuse.

Above all, one must avoid giving the impression that one has 'emotional baggage', or rather, 'issues' with men lest one is seen as 'damaged goods'. One must give the impression that one is 'innocent' about male domination or perhaps giggle about it all. The idea is that one must be emotionally and psychologically 'fresh'. The misogynistic term 'damaged goods' was once used to describe women who had sex before marriage. The word 'fresh' is a sex industry euphemism for 'virgin'. In their analysis of the seemingly liberated post-feminist genre of 'Chick Lit romance', Rosalind Gill and Elena Herdieckerhoff (2006) argue that heroines are 're-virginised':

> Interestingly, whatever their degree of sexual experience, heroines are 're-virginised' in the narrative when it comes to the encounter with their hero. With him, they return to what we might characterise as an emotionally virginal state, which wipes away previous sullying experiences ... (p. 13).

---

35 <http://www.yintegrity.com/blog/12-thing-a-woman-does-that-men-find-irresistible> (accessed 21 June 2013).

The cultural imperative to be emotionally 'fresh' can be understood as the mass 're-virginisation' of the female mind. The emotionally re-virginised girl-woman must hide grief and anger at oppression, pretending, as it were, that she has never been 'fucked over' by patriarchy, in order that she can sell herself as untouched by 'previous sullying experiences' with men. The re-virginised emotionally fresh femininity is the opposite of jaded, sexually *used* 'damaged goods' femininity. Or, as a popular *Sydney Morning Herald* dating discussion blog, Ask Sam, puts it (on the subject of 'When do you become "damaged goods"?'):

> One male friend defines it as 'anyone who's been in a long-term relationship before you start dating them' (which pretty much outlines the majority of the 30-something population!). Another defines it as a woman who's been married before, has kids, still talks to her ex and is cynical about men. A third says it's any woman who's been dumped, abused or cheated on.[36]

The idea that women are 'damaged goods' if they speak negatively about men is a form of common sense and central to the sexual politics of the new emotional ageism. Younger women, in this context, have more sexual worth, not only because they are physically younger but because they might be politically virginal about male oppression.

As a form of emotional engineering, the compulsory positive fresh girly attitude operates to mask vast amounts of chronic emotional pain and physical exploitation by punishing criticism of the patriarchal status quo. Affective ageism represents a tightening of the emotional straightjacket of patriarchy. Be happy, or spare us your revolting misery. As Sady Doyle writes in an article defending Tori Amos,

---

36 'When do you become "damaged goods"?' <http://blogs.smh.com.au/lifestyle/asksam/archives/2008/06/would_you_date_someone_who_is.html> (accessed 20 August 2013).

as a society, we encourage girls and women to be emotionally accessible, and in touch with their feelings; we say that it is an innately feminine trait. We say it, that is, until they have feelings that make us uncomfortable, at which point we recast them as melodramatic harpies, shrieking banshees, and basket cases.[37]

Although women are routinely accused of being too emotional, of being blubbering, screaming, complaining psychos, the range of permissible feelings for women is narrowing. The misogynistic accusation that women are too emotional contains a lie: women's emotions are heavily controlled by formal, and informal, stigmatising psychiatric labels. The comment, 'You're crazy' and its endless permutations, is a simple, and oppressively boring response to women who, as Doyle suggests, are emotionally disobedient. The brutal limitations placed on women's emotions, the pseudo-psychiatric judgements and labelling and the herding of women into therapy and psychiatry, calls attention to the fact that women are still the second sex, a sex that is denied the full range of human emotions.

Most find it difficult to perform the wide-eyed blank Powerpuff carefree confident girly ideal in a relentlessly abusive misogynistic culture.[38] Not surprisingly, Big Pharma, and its public relations division which most people understand as 'psychiatry', has helped things along with a vast and proliferating range of drugs for the female brain. Faking being an uncomplaining self-empowered little girl is so much easier if one is drugged. There are now a plethora of drugs on the market which supposedly enable women to reclaim the youthful

---

37 <http://bitchmagazine.org/article/birth-of-the-uncool> (accessed 21 July 2013).
38 *The Powerpuff Girls* (1998) is a cartoon about three girl power superheroes named Blossom, Bubbles and Buttercup who fly around with enormous smiling faces and oversized eyes defeating the forces of evil. See Krissy Naudus, 'Powerpuff Girls: A society of Girl Power' <http://www.urbangeek.net/writings/academic/powerpuff.html> (accessed 14 August 2013).

buoyant optimism and enthusiasm for life that they might have lost by being systematically oppressed. And if one is convinced that the only reason one cannot perform the compulsory girly confidence trick is because one has a defective brain, then what a relief it is to have one's brain corrected by drugs, which have been tested on rodents' brains in laboratories owned by multinational pharmaceutical companies.

2.3 Chemical Liberation: The 'Youthful' Brain

> 'You're doing much better,' Nurse Roditits said approvingly to Connie, and actually smiled. 'Now you want to get better.'
> 'Oh, yes.' She forced a stiff smile. 'I want to get well now.' War, she thought, I'm at war. No more fantasies, no more hopes. *War*.
> —Marge Piercy, *Woman on the Edge of Time* (1979/1985, p. 338).

Antidepressant drugs, reflects the psychiatrist and best-selling author Peter D. Kramer in *Listening to Prozac* (1997), are like a chemical makeover for the personality. Drawing on his case histories of depressed women, Kramer explores how, once dosed with drugs, women seem to float above their worries and become confident. "There is a sense," writes Kramer, "that antidepressants are ... liberating and empowering" (p. 40). His female patients report a "lack of responsibility for the injured" and a "loss of seriousness" (p. 9), becoming "vivacious and fun-loving" (p. 11), experiencing a restored child-like "capacity to play" (p. 21), less emotional sensitivity (p. 71), a "greater tolerance for teasing" by intimate male partners (p. 94), and an ability to block out sadistic mind games by intimate male partners (p. 104) which is described as "resilience" (p. 134). The women are also "able to forgive men's faults" (p. 147) and are "lightened" (p. 196). Kramer acknowledges that a particular kind of female personality is fashionable today and he ponders whether or not it is ethical to change women's personalities with drugs that he ultimately defends as enabling women's "chemical liberation." It also allows women to adapt to patriarchy and achieve heterosexual success. The personal and political consequences of all these manipulations are not mentioned.

It is no coincidence that the new Prozac personality is similar to the confident and playful girl power ideal. Prozac-induced femininity exudes positive 'youthfulness' and is not weighed down or burdened (aged) by seriousness and is strangely immune to the depressing impact of ubiquitous misogyny. Verbally abuse her, and she will probably giggle. At last, patriarchy has found a way of making women lighten up about being oppressed.

The psychiatric diagnosis of women is a profoundly political act. Numerous studies "demonstrate that women's feelings, thoughts and behaviours are more likely to be defined as madness than those of men. Being female is a risk factor for being labelled mad" (Williams, 1999, p. 36).[39] Diagnosing women with psychiatric problems is also a vastly profitable process for pharmaceutical corporations. As Linda Simoni-Wastila states: "It has also been reported that women are 48% more likely than men to use any psychotropic medication after statistically controlling for demographics, health status, economic status and diagnosis" (Simoni-Wastila, 2000, p. 289).

Not only are women drugged in record numbers but women are also brain damaged by electroconvulsive therapy (ECT, also known as electric shock treatment).[40] There is evidence that ECT permanently damages the entire brain but "probably more than 100,000 patients a year in the United States are electroshocked. The majority are women and many are elderly" (Breggin, 1998, p. 6). As feminist critics point out, psychiatry continues to be a method for enforcing oppressor-friendly behaviour in women (Chan et al., 2012; Agel, 1971).

---

39 See Beckwith (1993) and Broverman et al. (1970).
40 See, for example, <http://intcamp.wordpress.com/ect-women/> (accessed 21 July 2013) and also <http://chrysmassociates.blogspot.fr/2012/10/women-get-ect-in-scotland-twice-as-much.html> (accessed 21July 2013).

According to Dr David Muzina of the Medco Neuroscience Therapeutic Resource Center, "we also believe that [women] may be at higher risk for major depressive disorders. *It likely is biological.* We don't know exactly why" (in Bindley, 2011, my emphasis). The fascist idea that women are biologically inferior and mentally abnormal persists. Psychiatry identifies the female brain as defective and capitalist drug companies sell the cure to women.

Structurally entrenched misogyny is clearly the leading cause of women's global misery. However, patriarchal capitalism does not care about the suffering of women. The intense and prolonged—and all too often silenced—suffering of women is of interest to the system only insofar as it can extract profit from women's misery. Patriarchy is not interested in depressed women; it is only interested in *controlling* depressed women. And psychotropic drugs achieve this by damaging women's brains.

"The rat studies indicate that a variety of stressors can cause chemical and anatomical changes whose behavioural effects may not be apparent for some time," hints Kramer (1997 p. 118). Likewise, it is found that chemical and anatomical changes in the female human brain are caused by stress. Tortured rat brains, oppressed female brains: why bother considering the vast differences between rodent and human brains when it comes to marketing drugs to women? Today women are dosed with a 'cock-tale' of drugs that have been tested on rodent brains in order to conform to the desirable uncomplaining, positive and carefree youthful personality that is now required by patriarchy. The wounded brains of women are bathed in antidepressants. The drugged woman is liberated from seriousness.

Laboratory experiments have found that antidepressants create 'youthful' brains in mice. In a 2011 *Forbes* magazine article, 'The perfect marriage: Science begins to explain why antidepressants and talk therapy go hand in hand', it is reported that "antidepressants may indeed set the brain back to a more 'plastic' or youthful state" (Walton, 2011). The conclusion is based on rather sinister experiments with fluoxetine (Prozac) on the brains of tortured mice. The neurological experiments are part of a range of studies on the 'extinction' of Pavlovian fear conditioning or learned helplessness. Depression has long been argued to be a form of learned helplessness. Vast amounts of Big Pharma money is being spent on discovering the 'extinction' of learned helplessness.

In this experiment, first of all, the feet of mice are electrocuted when they hear a certain tone until they learn to freeze when they hear the tone in anticipation of being hurt again. The mice enter a state of learned helplessness. When the adult mice were given fluoxetine they unlearnt the connection between the tone and the electrocution and quickly stopped freezing with horror. The 'extinction' of Pavlovian fear conditioning has been achieved by drugging the mice with antidepressants.

The *Forbes* article gushes on merrily about the wonders of fluoxetine:

> As the researchers suspected, mice who were given fluoxetine during extinction behaved much more like young mice, in the ease with which they stopped reacting to the tone. And when they were reintroduced to the shock later on, they weren't so quick to fall back on their previously stressed behaviour. On the other hand, mice who were not given fluoxetine 'renewed' their fear response much more quickly upon getting shocked again … The brains of the mice who were treated with fluoxetine also looked 'younger' … If the mouse brain is acting like it's younger, more plastic, more open to new experiences when it's bathed in antidepressants, what does this means for human beings battling depression? … A more youthful-acting brain could learn new ways to cope, dealing with stressors, and instituting new thought patterns (Walton, 2011).

The majority of women, like the mice trapped in the drug company experiment, are confined in a woman-hating culture from which they cannot escape. They suffer continual shocks: verbal, sexual, emotional and physical abuse in and outside the home, pervasive social contempt, a sense of powerlessness and despair, and a lack of control over their ability to work effectively or even take care of their own children. Women's depression, as feminists have pointed out, is a logical and rational response to having one's human rights continually abused.[41] Depression, burn out, or learned helplessness can be compared to the ways in which the mice freeze when they hear the sound before their torture.

What patriarchy needs is a drug which can disconnect women's learnt response to their oppression so that they can 'find new ways to cope' by erasing what they have already learnt about a woman-hating environment.

The learned helplessness of the tortured mice is apparently cured by antidepressants and this is heralded as a liberating breakthrough (for women, especially, as women are the largest consumers of antidepressants).[42] But another way of interpreting this experiment is that the residual survival instincts are being eliminated, or to use the official terminology: the 'extinction' of Pavlovian fear conditioning has been achieved. The new chemically enhanced mouse brain is 'youthful' or 'plastic', in the sense that it has forgotten what it had learnt. It has become 'innocent'. It no longer acts on self-protective instincts that have been developed over time which warn about danger. In the experiment, the self-protective instincts of adult mice are all but broken by antidepressants.

---

41 See, for example, Radloff (1975), Chesler (1972), Stoppard (2000), Beauboeuf-Lafontant (2007).

42 Peter Wehrwein writes that in America "23% of women in their 40s and 50s take antidepressants, a higher percentage than any other group (by age or sex)" <http://www.health.harvard.edu/blog/astounding-increase-inantidepressant-use-by-americans-201110203624> (accessed 14 August).

2.4 From the Fist to the Pill

Disciplining and controlling girls and women with violence is no longer officially permissible in the west—but male violence continues to destroy and kill large numbers of girls and women every day. But, more importantly for patriarchal capitalism, male violence towards women is not profitable: in fact, it costs governments a lot of money. Broken bones and beaten up bodies require expensive medical care, time off from housework, school, child care and paid work, perhaps welfare payments, funding for women's refuges and, occasionally, costly police and court resources. Moreover, physical violence is not a very effective way of controlling women; it usually has to be done repeatedly, women often become depressed and 'dysfunctional' wage slaves, sexual partners, mothers, house-wives, and sometimes escape and make costly trouble.

There are other more sophisticated and profitable ways of disciplining and controlling women that directly damage the brain without lifting a fist or raising a voice. Women can now be disciplined and controlled with psychiatric pills, subjected to a chemical beating that they themselves pay for and swallow for their own good. Once a woman has been persuaded that her brain is defective (that the problem is, literally, inside her own head; that she has a 'chemical imbalance' in her brain and it's all her fault), she is expected to take responsibility for herself by correcting the defect with psychiatric pills. She pays money to misogynistic pharmaceutical corporations so that she can gain 'control' over her life and no longer be the 'victim' of her emotions. She has been liberated from being 'too serious'. She must take her pills in the name of responsibility to herself and those around her.

The disciplinary impact of violence against women leaves bruises, wounds, damaged organs, broken bones, punctured eardrums, lost vision, broken minds, terrified children. The chemical punishment and control of women leaves no external signs of abuse—there is only an internal bio-chemical wounding; adverse effects that require more pills which in turn often have other, more serious adverse effects. The visible marks of domination, the bruises, breaks, wounds and tears, are replaced by the silent daily swallowing of drugs. Violence against women is something misogynists do to women to discipline and control them; chemical control, on the other hand, is marketed as a type of feminist self-empowerment. As Kramer suggests, antidepressants are "feminist drugs" (1997, p. 40). They are also drugs that make women more pleasing to men and a male-dominated workplace, less difficult, critical, demanding, high-maintenance, needy, angry; and more relaxed, placid, and easy to be with. The anti-psychiatry movement accurately describes antidepressants as *chemical lobotomies*.[43] The psychiatrist Peter R. Breggin has drawn on extensive evidence to argue that psychiatric drugs damage the brain, a condition that he terms "psychiatric drug-induced Chronic Brain Impairment" or CBI (Breggin, 2011). Drugs that stop the normal activity of the frontal lobe and retard and suppress general mental functioning are effectively disabling the brain.

The symptoms of Chronic Brain Impairment include short-term memory loss, concentration problems, indifference and emotional numbness, loss of empathy, weight gain, headaches, dizziness, dry mouth, appetite disturbances, palpitations, suicidal ideation and actions, high blood pressure, tremors, loss of libido and insomnia. Antidepressants do not make you happy. Rather, they numb feelings; one is emptied out, leaving only the social demand to act positive without the interference of conflicting negative emotions. It is easier to adopt the mask of positive youthfulness when one is chemically lobotomised.

Such is the hegemonic power of psychiatry that diagnosing women with psychiatric disorders has become the casual

---

43 Such drugs have long been recognised as a form of chemical lobotomy. See, for example, <http://www.sntp.net/drugs/thorazine.htm> (accessed 12 August 2013).

sport of a woman-hating culture. 'Psycho', 'crazy', 'hysterical' and the more subtle and pernicious 'emotional', 'needy', 'co-dependent', 'low self-esteem', 'insecure', 'negative' or 'victim', are judgments about women's character which are all caught up in the psychiatric control of women's lives. Most women are frequently labelled 'insane' for expressing their misery and failing to act positive. It is a form of misogynistic abuse that is also about pushing women towards the doctor's room, the the-rapist's couch, and the chemist.

Borderline Personality Disorder (BPD) entered the Diagnostic and Statistical Manual of Mental Disorders (DSM) in 1980 (Friedel, 2004). Studies have produced evidence that diagnosed BPD "is more common in women than in men (about 70% and 30% respectively)" (Lieb *et al.*, 2004). Numerous studies have examined the brains of the diagnosed, and argue that "structural and functional neuroimaging has revealed a dysfunctional network of brain regions" in particular a "dysfunctional fronto-limbic network" and "reduced hippocampal and amygdala volumes" (Lieb *et al.*, 2004, p. 455). This *Lancet* article continues:

> Simultaneous limbic and prefrontal disturbances suggest dual brain pathology as a neuropathological correlate of hyperarousal-dyscontrol syndrome, seen in patients with borderline personality disorder. However, whether the observed neurobiological dysfunctions are pre-existing—i.e. due to genetic, pre-postnatal factors, or adverse events during childhood—or the consequence of the disorder itself, is unknown.

The central point here is that the brains of people with Borderline Personality Disorder are 'dysfunctional', inferior, weird, defective and abnormal.

Significantly, however, the article states that "high proportions of patients with this disorder are continuously taking medication and rates of intensive polypharmacy are not uncommon, and do not decline with time" (p. 457). People who are diagnosed with BPD are often treated with neuroleptics. One side effect of such drugs is tardive dyskinesia, rapid and uncontrollable whole body repetitive movements that ripple continuously through the face and the rest of the body. *Tardive dyskinesia is a symptom of brain damage.*[44] Neuroleptics disrupt the function of the frontal lobe causing a chemical lobotomy. And yet, the logical possibility that the abnormalities discovered in the studies of patients' brains might be the result of 'psychiatric drug-induced Chronic Brain Impairment' (Breggin, 2011) is completely marginalised. Meanwhile, brain-damaging anti-depressants, antipsychotics and mood-stabilising drugs are pre-scribed, but there "are no guidelines for preventing BPD."[45]

As many feminists have argued, BPD can also be seen as a list of behaviours that annoy misogynists (Shaw, 2005). Consider the Wikipedia entry for BPD:

> People with BPD feel emotions more easily, more deeply, and for longer than others do. For instance, while an emotion typically fires for 12 seconds, it can last up to 20 percent longer in people with BPD. Moreover, emotions in people with BPD might repeatedly re-fire, or reinitiate, prolonging their emotional reactions even further. Consequently, it can take a long time for people with BPD to return to a stable emotional baseline following an intense emotional experience.

Are women's emotions now so tightly controlled that they are only permitted to feel anything for *12 seconds* before they risk being diagnosed with a psychiatric illness? BPD is a feminine mental illness, apparently, but it also provides insights into the new emotional fascism of misogyny.

---

44 For a short bibliography of articles on tardive dyskinesia brain damage see <http://www.mindfreedom.org/kb/psychiatric-drugs/antipsychotics/neuroleptic-brain-damage/mosherbibliography> (accessed 15 August 2013).

45 <http://en.wikipedia.org/wiki/Borderline_personality_disorder> (accessed 21 July 2013).

The Wikipedia entry continues:

> While strongly desiring intimacy, people with BPD tend toward insecure, avoidant or ambivalent, or fearfully preoccupied attachment patterns in relationships, and they often view the world as generally dangerous and malevolent. BPD is linked to increased levels of chronic stress and conflict in romantic relationships, decreased satisfaction of romantic partners, abuse and unwanted pregnancy. However, these factors appear to be linked to personality disorders in general.

Women's experience of oppression has been neatly pathologised. And it is hardly surprising that the Internet is saturated with websites full of misogynistic warnings about managing and avoiding 'psycho' BPD girls and women.

The incessant, punishing demand that women disguise their suffering with the mask of a positive girly personality (with the 'help' of a *chemical lobotomy* if necessary) signals that one key feature of a re-loaded misogyny is a war against women's emotions. Women do not participate in the new ageism because they have low self-esteem, or are shallow or narcissistic. Failure to have a youthful face and body and a youthfully positive attitude often results in a dangerous loss of income and increasingly cruel forms of social marginalisation and vilification. The triumph of the new ageism depends upon the neo-liberal destruction of safety nets that enabled women to have a minimal level of autonomous survival. Behind the mask of individual compliantly positive youthfulness there is an old burning rage waiting to collectivise.

3.0 Rape Becomes Lulz

A world without rapists would be a world in which women moved freely without fear of men. That some men rape provides a sufficient threat to keep all women in a constant state of intimidation, forever conscious of the knowledge that the biological tool must be held in awe, for it may turn to weapon with sudden swiftness born of harmful intent ... Rather than society's aberrants or 'spoilers of purity', men who commit rape have served in effect as front-line masculine shock troops, terrorist guerrillas in the longest battle the world has ever known.

—Susan Brownmiller, *Against Our Will: Men, Women and Rape*
(1975, p. 15)

Living in a rape culture means adjusting to being hyper-vigilant about male violence to the point where risk management becomes second nature. It means living with the continuum of male sexual violence on a daily basis, from creepy and threatening looks and comments in the street, home and workplace, to online rape threats, attempted assault and actual assault. It means inhabiting a paradoxical space where the rape and murder of women is prohibited but everywhere eroticised and the object of laughter.

To take just one example of rape culture, the globally popular American fantasy series *Game of Thrones* features a blond child bride being continually raped by her warlord husband. "But it's all ok because a prostitute slave teaches the thirteen-year-old princess super sexy sex skills, and she proceeds to blow the warlord's mind so throughly [*sic*] that they fall in love," notes feminist Laurie Penny (2012).[46]

Many men, when asked a simple question about why male domination exists, reply that it is because men are stronger than women. This answer seems innocuously simple-minded, but the explanatory statement that 'men have power over women because they are physically stronger than women' also means 'men can rape and kill women if they want to'. There is no point replying that it is illegal to rape and kill women. The law does not come into it at all. It is as though the legal prohibitions against male sexual violence are little more than the sales pitch of a corporation eager to hide its criminal intent behind images of satisfied customers.

The majority of victims do not report, and the majority of rapists walk free (Miller *et al.*, 2011; Fayard and Rocheron, 2011; Belknap, 2010).[47] As the title of a 2013 article by Nigel Morris in *The Independent* puts it: '100,000 assaults. 1,000 rapists sentenced. Shockingly low conviction rates revealed. Latest statistics also show difficulties in persuading victims to report attacks'.[48] Although media attention on particular rapes

---

46 For some discussions about the sexual politics of the ultra-violent *Game of Thrones* see <https://medium.com/the-t-v-age/ec8767758cda>, <https://medium.com/the-t-v-age/ec8767758cda> and <http://jezebel.com/game-of-boners-this-is-torture-porn-504821180> (accessed 15 August 2013).

47 Nicole Fayard and Yvette Rocheron write:
   Today sexual violence is seen as one of the worst possible crimes; 'the consequence of rape is no longer immorality but psychic death; it is no longer a question of debauchery but of the shattering of identity, an incurable wound to which the victim seems doomed'. As this position is widely accepted in many countries, why is it that rape victims continue to fail to obtain reparation by the courts? This remains the case in France and England & Wales (Vigarello, 2001, p. 244 cited in Fayard and Rocheron, 2011, p. 68).

48 To quote the article: "Only 1,070 rapists are convicted every year despite up to 95,000 people—the vast majority of them women—suffering the trauma of rape—according to the new research by the Ministry of Justice, the Home Office and the Office for National Statistics." See also <http://www.theguardian.

occasionally stirs up public debate, these rapes are the exception
to the norm simply because victims have broken their silence
and the criminal justice system has been involved. One cannot
but wonder how many people know of, or are friends with,
men who have sexually assaulted women and children, and yet
do nothing about it.

It has only been since the 1960s and 1970s that most
western women have been able to work outside the home without needing permission from their husbands/owners. It is only
in the last few decades that marital rape has been recognised in
some nations as a human rights violation. In Australia marital
rape was outlawed as late as 1991 (Temkin, 2002).[49] As late as
1993 the United Nations published the Declaration on the
Elimination of Violence Against Women. In many countries
young girls are still forced to marry their rapists.

Raping women and children continues to be a lethal
form of oppression in advanced neo-liberal democracies.
Victims of male sexual violence continue to be branded as
'damaged goods' and re-abused in the criminal justice system
to such an extent that the majority of victims simply give up
and opt out of the legal process (Fisher *et al.*, 2000; Fisher *et
al.*, 2003). Lawyers are often reluctant to take on rape cases
because they know they are difficult to win. Child victims of
male sexual violence are subjected to ritualistic humiliation in
courts (Taylor, 2004). Child pornography victims are subjected
to malicious attacks by bourgeois academics in high-ranking
American legal journals (Lollar, 2012).

Young women, who sustain the majority of sexual assaults,
not only endure court-licensed abuse, but they are now also

com/society/2013/jun/20/one-in-three-women-suffers-violence> (accessed 15
August 2013). See also Hallet (2011).

49 See also <http://www.intlawgrrls.com/2012/08/in-australia-reconsidering-marital-
rape.html> (accessed 15 August 2013). "In 1991, in its judgment in *R v L*, the
High Court of Australia made a declaration that the 'marital rape immunity' was
no longer part of the common law of Australia."

bullied online for daring to speak out. Raped girls are urged to kill themselves by pack verbal abuse that is all too often uttered as mocking jokes (Salek, 2013). Victim-blaming has become lethal.

In a novel by feminist academic Yvette Rocheron, *Double Crossings* (2009), a mother decides to commit suicide after she is brutally raped by a cousin, knowing that, if she lives, the crime will destroy her family and her life. "For her loved ones, a sublime act of love ... She would go down knowingly ... [T]he vitriolic defacement of women, the misguided abortions, the rapes. She was a thousand years old" (p. 271). There is no humour in this novel as the mother leaps to her death, merely a solemn awareness of the barbarism of a crime against women that leaves the murderous poison of social death in her body.

I have lost count of how many women—friends, students, colleagues, relatives, and acquaintances—have told me they have been raped. All of the rapists have gotten away with it while the women are burdened with years of unspeakable shame and self-hatred, or shunned by their families for daring to speak out about male relatives who raped them. The stories involve horrendous child sexual abuse, rape at knifepoint, abductions in vans, group rapes, women being drugged and raped, rapes by colleagues, partners and ex-partners. A woman who was raped by her grandfather told me recently that it took her 30 years to understand that her body belonged to her. Another woman, a feminist activist and journalist, after going public about being raped at knifepoint, was subjected to online abuse along the lines that she should be 'raped with a box cutter'. When I read the comment about the box cutter it took a few moments to sink in that the man who had posted the comment was saying that he wanted to butcher her vagina with a knife. Not surprisingly, many women keep quiet about being sexually assaulted. And all of this occurs in a world in which women who speak out about male sexual violence, or any form of male domination, are routinely subjected to online rape threats (Lewis, 2011). Again, the majority of threats never result in prosecution and women are often told to 'get over it', 'toughen up' or 'lighten up' or have sex with a man. 'She just needs a good fuck', is how the all too familiar saying goes ... Oddly, having sex with men is meant to dispel fear of being raped, as though women who have an accurate assessment of the dangers of rape culture are hysterics who just need sex. The idea that women enjoy being raped still persists (Suarez and Gadalla, 2010); and if women are assumed to enjoy being raped then their protests about being harmed by rape can easily be reduced to a farce.

3.1 Sexual Violence against Women Is So Funny Right Now

Rape culture is rape jokes, rape culture is rape jokes on t-shirts, rape jokes in college newspapers, rape jokes in soldiers' home videos, rape jokes on the radio, rape jokes on news broadcasts, rape jokes in magazines, rape jokes in viral videos, rape jokes in promotions for children's movies, rape jokes on page Six (and again!), rape jokes on the funny pages, rape jokes on TV shows, rape jokes on the campaign trail, rape jokes on Halloween, rape jokes in online content by famous people, rape jokes in online content by non-famous people, rape jokes in headlines, rape jokes onstage at clubs, rape jokes in politics, rape jokes in one-woman shows, rape jokes in print campaigns, rape jokes in movies, rape jokes in cartoons, rape jokes in nightclubs, rape jokes on MTV, rape jokes on late-night chat shows, rape jokes in tattoos, rape jokes in stand-up comedy, rape jokes on websites, rape jokes at award shows, rape jokes in online contests, rape jokes in movie trailers, rape jokes on the side of busses, rape jokes on cultural institutions ...[50]

Imagine a white-dominated nation saturated with jokes about destroying black people. We would, I think, have no hesitation is calling that culture fascist. We would probably understand the incessant joking about violence against black people as the

---

50 <http://sarahgetscritical.com/> (accessed 23 July 2012).

celebratory laughter of a sadistic white supremacist culture. And it is easy to recognise the gestures of violent oppression in the Nazi ridiculing of Jewish people during the 12 years of Hitler's rule (1933–1945): the cruel caricature of Jewish bodies and minds was a dehumanising tactic. And if someone instructed us to think of this dehumanising laughter as merely a bad-taste joke, or the boisterous humour of unrefined individuals which had no connection whatsoever to the systematic violent oppression of the very people whose suffering is being laughed at, we would recognise their argument as an apology for mass violence.

The sexual degradation of women has long been accompanied by laughter. If misogyny has a soundtrack it is canned laughter. Invented by the American Charles R. Douglas in the 1950s, canned laughter first became popular in the *I Love Lucy* television comedy about the oppression of a wife by her husband. The husband commands the wife to obey him—"And that's an order!"—as canned laughter instructs us that his unapologetic domination is hilarious. As she is spanked for failing to obey him, canned laughter informs us that this is funny. In the episode 'Equal Rights' the husband says: "I am the first one to agree that women should have all the rights they want. As long as they stay in their place."[51] Laughter again instructs the audience that it is not only permissible to laugh at the oppression of women but that it is expected. Women's human rights are transformed into a long-winded farce. Replace the canned laughter with the soundtrack from a horror film and the contempt for women seems rather more ominous.

The internationally popular British 1970s comedy *The Benny Hill Show* is awash with scenes of sexual assault that are accompanied by canned laughter. Scantily-clad women run desperately from rapists to the sound of the Benny Hill 'Yakety

---

51 <http://www.youtube.com/watch?v=1nx6BsYIvU4> (accessed 9 September 2013).

Sax' 'chase scene' soundtrack. Rape culture turns sexual assault into a farce with canned laughter and an upbeat soundtrack. During the same era the popular British *Carry On* films also mocked sexual assault with canned laughter. The machismo laughter offers an implicit challenge: you are either laughing with us or you are against us. To refuse to laugh at women's oppression is to risk being marginalised as a humourless bore.

The exploitation, objectification and degradation of women in pornography also pass as humour. The 1972 pornography classic *Deep Throat* is a comedy about a woman who has a clitoris at the back of her throat and is advised by her doctor to perform oral sex on numerous men. Yet it was far from funny for Linda Boreman (aka Linda Lovelace) who testified in 1986 that "virtually every time someone watches that movie, they're watching me being raped."[52] Today there are websites called 'Humor on' which advertise "hardcore porn, bizarre porn and shocking videos." Hardcore pornography websites are frequently passed off as shockingly funny. The difference between the 1970s Benny Hill comedy of sexual assault and contemporary rape jokes is that the laughter has taken on the cruelty of hardcore porn.

Since the mid-1990s 'rape' has become a loosely applied verb, which describes the conquest, use and abuse of anything from a McDonald's burger to a maths test: 'I raped that burger', 'I raped that test', and so on. Transformed by the alchemy of macho-slang, the entire world becomes something to be raped. Girls and women are also often described as worthy or unworthy of rape—'I'd rape her' or 'she's not worth raping' or 'you'd have to pay me to rape her'. Or men might say that a computer game 'raped' them, meaning they lost. Just as the word and concept of rape has been emptied out of meaning, becoming a cool throwaway line, raping women has become

---

52 <https://againstpornography.org/reallindalovelace.html> (accessed 21 July 2013).

a source of humour. Images of violent rape are the erotic slapstick of the new sexual fascism.

The word 'rape'—a key concept in the political language of feminism—has been colonised by patriarchy at the same time that sexual violence against women has been invisibilised by the upwardly mobile term 'gender-based sexual violence' (GBSV) (Hawthorne, 2004). *Woman, women,* words that are already colonised by the words *man* and *men,* have now disappeared into *gender,* a word which appears to include women but which, given the manifest power differences between the sexes, functions to make way for the rights of men as though these rights have to be fought for. Gender is to sexism as woman is to misogyny. Sexism and gender are male-friendly neo-liberal words. "Won't somebody please think of the men?" because they are, apparently, equal to women in their oppression by sexism and gender. The male elite of the new world order are actually victims of heterosexual masculinity. It would make equally as much sense to replace 'white supremacy' with the concept of 'racially-based discrimination', or 'ruling class oppression' with the concept of 'economically-based prejudice'. The tactic is about obscuring forms of violence which, despite the laboriously pompous deconstructions of identity politics, are still identity based. It also provides an opportunity for the oppressors and those who do their bidding to silence and accuse, for example, a poor, non-white lesbian for being sexist and racist when she speaks back to white male heterosexual power.

At the heart of the cultural war over the resurgence of rape culture is the politics of laughter. Rape humour has become the preferred hiding place of a new form of control that is everywhere supported by the serious machinery of institutionalised oppression. Rape propaganda passes as humour and defends itself with opportunistic appeals to freedom of speech. "Now those dreary feminists and affili-ated authoritarian bores want to destroy our right to laugh!"

comes the outraged self-pitying reply. The women's liberation movement has always been accused of lacking a sense of humour, and attacks on women's basic human rights have long passed as humour. Laughing at the oppression of women is the best medicine for those who fear being laughed at. Meanwhile women are encouraged to laugh at themselves in order to cure themselves of serious political insights. One must be ready to signal one's allegiance to male supremacy at any time through a derisive smirk, a rolling of the eyes, a contemptuous dismissal accompanied by a short laugh, or an abusive comment made with a smile and a harsh, cold guffaw. The laughter surrounding the violent oppression of women is the echo of a new authoritarian masculinity that passes itself off as an anti-authoritarian rebellion against the imagined triumph of 'political correctness', aka feminism.

The proudly infamous 'Rape Sloth' meme is just one example of this cruel zeitgeist. An image from a Terry Richardson Pirelli photo shoot of a sloth next to a model's ear, its long claws reaching towards her neck, now carries hundreds of rape jokes. Here are a few of them:

> I take the 'the' out of psychotherapist.
> Go ahead, call the cops. They can't unrape you.
> You better not pout, you better not cry. You better not scream, I'm going in dry.
> You know what's the best thing about twenty-six-year-olds? There are twenty of them.
> Go ahead, call the cops. See who cums first.
> You know what really turns me on? Struggle.
> This joke is going to be forced. Just like our sex.
> I like people like I like my wine. 12-years-old and locked in my basement.
> I use pepperspray as lubricant.
> It's not necrophilia if you were alive when I started.
> Do you have a sewing machine? Cuz I'm gonna tear dat ass up.[53]

---

53 <http://www.quickmeme.com/rape-sloth/?upcoming> (accessed 21 July 2013).

It would be a mistake to dismiss these jokes as the puerile slobber of emasculated nerds. Rape humour has become widespread to the point of banality.

In October 2011 members of the Yale University fraternity house, Delta Kappa Epsilon, felt entitled to chant: "No Means Yes, Yes Means Anal" (Rosenfeld, 2011, p. 41). Again, this was considered a joke. Many teenagers have told me that anti-rape campaigns are the subject of widespread jokes and that appearing serious about rape is uncool, even though most knew of a girl who had been raped. Rape jokes are common in cyberspace as well, and much of the hardcore pornography is framed as a kind of shock and awe humour, as a kind of psychological medicine designed to toughen up their consumers. A student told me how she was invited into the living room of her share-house where a group of young men were laughing at some bestiality pornography. She was expected to laugh at the woman who was being sodomised by a donkey. Men's urinals in the shape of women's lips pass as humour. T-shirts emblazoned with pro-rape jokes are 'funny'. One is expected to laugh at computer games where women are raped and slaughtered.

Rape as slapstick gains cultural currency by passing as subversive, edgy, oppositional and counter-cultural. On the surface the laughter seems to belong to the tradition of a carnivalesque subversion, where the law and authority are mocked and inverted, exaggerated and undermined by icono-clastic gestures. Yet it is an ultra-conservative misogyny that endows rape jokes with the halo of earthy authenticity. What is falsely imagined to be the boringly earnest sentimentalism of straight mainstream morality is targeted as repressive. Indeed 'morality' has become code for all that must be fought against if free speech and democracy are to be defended.

Attempts at hipster irony pervade cultural critiques of feminist work that calls attention to the violation of women's human rights. The preferred attitude is a mocking, ironic laughter along with the solemn accusation that feminist protests about the resurgence of rape culture are dreary humourless neo-conservative moral panics. Indeed, beneath the accusation of 'moral panic' that has been flung at feminism since the 1970s, lurks the accusation that feminists lack a sense of humour and are unable to appreciate the subtle inter-textual irony that is meant to pervade postmodern consumer culture and which all consumers and readers (no matter how young) are assumed to be hip to. Everyone, it seems, is in on the joke except for feminists, and the joke, as they say, is on them. Yet, the real irony is that a postmodern reading that would, predictably, claim Benny Hill rape jokes as subversive deconstructions of post-war white British lower-middle-class heterosexual masculinity, and perhaps re-signify the whole thing in a display of self-consciously elitist textual performances bloated with gate-keeping postmodern jargon, remains obedient to the old ruling bourgeois disgust with compassion. Although some aspects of postmodernism might argue for remaining open to the unknowable singularity of the difference of 'the other', a mannered tolerance for alterity soon scrambles back into a lofty disdain when 'the other' speaks back about the structurally enforced oppression caused by patriarchy, capitalism and imperialism. Or as a white heterosexual upper-middle-class male Western Australian Professor said to me with a nasty laugh in 2010: "How can you bear to teach women's studies, it's just so stupid!"

The cruel laughter of misogyny that now echoes around us is more honest than the commercial sentimentalising of heterosexual love. While the cultural industries celebrate romantic love between men and women in a thousand films and songs, off-screen love for women is barely tolerated, or viewed as a fake mask adopted by lovers and partners in the competitive bourgeois game of social approval. Loving women goes against the cult of sadism which demands of men that they harden their emotions towards women in order to win resources. In this respect, the sadistic contempt for women, the refusal of compassion, pity, or empathy which is expressed as laughter, is far from an original break with a repressive past. It is merely the continuation of instrumental bourgeois morality which views sexual partners through the cold eyes of a banker calculating profit and loss. If marrying for love alone was a vice, now having a sexual partner for love alone is a vice. One must be pragmatic. Those who feel less win. Authentic healthy feelings are hard and cruel, driven by a calculating rationality, and all else is weakness, a symptom of failure, psychological and physical abnormality. And how better to demonstrate one's fitness for competition in a male supremacist culture than laughing at women's abject oppression?

Telling rape jokes, or laughing at women being brutalised has become a sign of virility and a marker of masculine freedom. In this context, raping women becomes a status-enhancing smashing of the feminising legal restraints imposed on male sexuality. The trending of rape jokes on the Internet also gains cool currency precisely because the Internet is seen as a feral outlaw social technology, an anarchic carnival space where every kind of subversion is permitted and defended in the name of freedom of speech—for those men who have access to the playground, at least.

Lulz culture, which uses new technologies to play malicious pranks, is pro-rape. The Urban Dictionary's top definition of 'lulz' which had 6,304 thumbs up by 30 May 2013 is: "[T]he one good reason to do anything, from trolling to rape. After every action taken you must make the epilogic dubious disclaimer: 'I did it for the lulz'."[54] Lulz emerged in the not-so-underground sub-cultures of the Internet in websites such as Dramatica Encyclopedica that promote online trolling as a cool lifestyle. The rape sloth meme is a form of lulz, aimed

---

54 <http://www.urbandictionary.com/define.php?term=lulz> accessed 21 July 2013).

at provoking an imaginary audience of moral bores while also bonding through humour with other cool pro-rape dudes.

Feminist blogger Sarahgetscritical names it the "'LULZ RAPE YO' so-called banter in my generation." She links the raping of an unconscious 16-year-old girl by the Steubenville jocks to the new lulz approach to rape. The jocks exchanged photographs of her unconscious body and made the following type of jokes:

> 'Let's just put a wagon in her butthole'. 'Is she going to feel it?' LOL HILARITY ENSUES. 'Why isn't she waking up?' EVEN MORE HILARITY. 'She's deader than a doornail. That's how you know she'd dead, cos someone PISSED on her'.[55]

Uploading images of females being raped is trending. One mainstream (in the sense that it was easily accessible) 2008 hardcore pornography website called Passed Out Pussy boasts:

> [O]ur specialty is young girls drunk or drugged before they are brutally abused … Some guys help a girl home when she has had to [sic] much to drink. We say, call your friends, bring out the camera and then take turns to fuck that drunk slut to a pulp!! (Bray, 2009).

This is meant to be funny. The website, which contained hundreds of images of girls being brutally raped, encouraged male consumers to share their rape videos. In an era in which almost everything is uploaded, it is not surprising that rapes are being circulated on the Internet.

In June 2013 the UK charity Rape Crisis stated that in the previous year an increasing number of victims had reported being filmed and subjected to further threats that their rapes will be posted online.[56] Pro-rape lulz culture is also about

---

55 <http://sarahgetscritical.com/?s=lulz> (accessed 21 July 2013).

56 <http://www.dailymail.co.uk/news/article-2338307/Rape-victims-terrified-videos-horrific-ordeals-postedonline-reported-surge-crime.html> (accessed 22 July 2013).

shaming and silencing victims. The girls probably know that if their rapes are made public online, they will be subjected to an avalanche of intense online and offline bullying and verbal abuse.

Rape jokes are very far from rebellious, subversive, or oppositional. They are fascist salutes to male supremacy. Laughing about the sexual (and thus the physical, emotional and psychological) torture of females, signals one's servile obedience to the misogynistic status quo. As Frank observes, "commercial fantasies of rebellion, liberation, and outright 'revolution' against the stultifying demands of mass society are commonplace almost to the point of invisibility in advertising, movies, and television programming" (1997, p. 4). The laughter that accompanies rape jokes is as thoughtful and spontaneous as canned laughter; it is the laugh track to the scripted sitcom of misogyny, where every violation of women's rights becomes an audience cue for a derisive laugh. Her screams and struggle, emotional and mental destruction, vomiting and blood, her mangled body, are greeted with laughter.

As one blogger puts it, "rape culture is a culture where people who have survived a violent crime are asked to laugh about it because other people think it's funny."[57] That victims are under pressure to laugh about being subjected to physical, sexual, emotional and psychological torture is chilling. Torture becomes slapstick. One must be fun. Don't be boring. Don't be so sensitive. One must avoid presenting oneself as a victim at all costs or risk dangerous levels of social death.[58] Transform your oppression into a source of entertainment for the masters. Or, if possible, eroticise your torture so that after they've laughed

---

57 <http://deadwildroses.wordpress.com/2013/06/15/%E2%80%8Erape-culture-is-a-culture-in-which-people-who-have-survived-a-violent-crime-are-asked-to-laugh-about-it-because-other-people-think-its-funny> (accessed 21 July 2013).

58 See Caroline S. Taylor, *Social Death*, Spinifex Press (forthcoming).

they can settle down to masturbate over it. Slut, whore, ho, bitch, slag, cum dumpster. LOL.

Misogyny has become a form of *emotional capital* which now circulates across all fields in overt and covert forms. Misogynistic contempt for women signifies the conquest of pity, compassion, and empathy, those weakening sentimental emotions that have no place in a ruthlessly competitive and militarised capitalist macho culture. Women too can purchase emotional capital by hating women. Indeed, hating women becomes a key way of warding off the threat of loss of erotic capital that occurs when one criticises men or displays critical emotions. But if one wants to appear cool one must express hatred of women lightly, as a joke, as something that invites others to laugh. Even if the joke might involve descriptions of children being raped or rapes so brutal that they result in the death of the woman ...

A white, blond Western Australian woman in her mid-twenties posts onto Facebook Inc. images of naked women with beer bottles inserted into their anuses to the applause of both sexes. She makes regular woman-hating jokes that in turn lead to more woman-hating jokes in the comments. She is popular, posts numerous erotic 'selfies', boasts about how often she goes out and how many drugs she takes, and knows how to please her Facebook Inc. crowd. And the irony is that all of this, which is very common in social networking websites, is presented as radical, as cool, rebellious and edgy, when the dreary reality is that it is conformity to an oppressive regime which long ago marketed hatred of women as a socially-approved attitude for both men and women.

A male blogger, defending the Rape Sloth meme, writes that taking offence at these rape jokes is a 'choice' and that attempts to censor or control what people find amusing is a violation of free speech. "'Rape Sloth'" is the "hot new meme buying all your drinks at the moment," he writes.

If you do not find 'Rape Sloth' funny, by all means exercise your freedom by choosing not to indulge in his lechery; but for freedom's sake, don't try to decide what other people find funny, because that is not something you can control. And since you can't control it, try finding something to laugh about. I strongly suggest 'Rape Sloth'.[59]

By implication, those who don't find rape jokes funny are censorious bores. Especially women who are expected to laugh at male jokes and smile with tolerance at all this naughty boyish humour. No one likes a serious female. According to the opportunistic logic of misogyny, pro-rape propaganda is merely the freedom to laugh. Laughing at politically incorrect jokes is meant to symbolise transcendence over conformity, a sign that one is too cool and smart for boring old-school politics.

Feminist activists have begun to resist the rise of rape culture on social media networks. On 29 May 2013 a watchdog.net petition circulated with the words:

Facebook regularly bans pictures of women breastfeeding or showing scars from mastectomies—but it's got no problem ignoring the posts that promote violence against women for months or dismissing them altogether.

Hating a religious or ethnic group gets you banned on Facebook, so why doesn't hating women? Join us in calling on Facebook to start treating this misogyny seriously and take these awful images and video down as soon as possible.

FACEBOOK PETITION: Hate speech can be misogynistic as well as racist. We call on you to stop ignoring pro-rape and pro-abuse posts and to take down video of women being assaulted the moment it's reported, not weeks after the fact.[60]

---

59 <http://newmediarockstars.com/2013/04/rape-sloth-is-the-last-meme-you-want-driving-you-home-gallery/> (accessed 12 July 2013).

60 <http://www.change.org/petitions/demand-facebook-remove-pages-that-promote-sexual-violence> (accessed 3 July 2013).

The petition had an impact and Facebook Inc. promised to try harder. But unfortunately, this very protest itself was derided as a joke, and further proof that feminists lack a sense of humour.

Recent popular 'feminist' protests against rape culture have not been as serious, however. In the SlutWalk protest marches that began in Canada in 2011, and soon spread to other western nations, women attempted to reclaim the word 'slut' by marching dressed as 'sluts' with 'no means no' and 'still not asking for it' slogans painted on their bodies or held up as signs. Part of the post-feminist pro-sex movement which frequently supports the divisive splitting of the women's liberation movement into anti- or pro-sex battles, the SlutWalk protests offered the world titillating images of young (and often white and middle-class) women flashing their knickers at rape culture. That black women have not felt compelled to perform 'NiggerWalks' dressed as housemaids or prostitutes is telling.[61] Moreover, it is hard not to notice that the SlutWalks have usurped the solemn grieving of Reclaim the Night marches with a self-consciously humorous attitude. Laughter, and not tears of grief for raped and murdered girls and women, accompanies SlutWalk.

In Brisbane, Australia, SlutWalk was sponsored by the Sex Party, a try-hard opportunistic libertarian group that promotes prostitution and pornography with cheerfully repetitive neo-liberal rhetoric about choice and individual freedom. This alliance alone suggests a deeply compromised movement. If SlutWalk is about challenging rape culture, it seems to have forgotten that the majority of women are raped not by strangers who approach them in the streets when they are wearing sexy clothes, but by men they know, too often relatives or partners, in their homes, wearing any kind of clothes. Although the marches promote themselves as a new diverse form of feminist activism, the understanding of rape culture is narrow. Men rape

---

61   See Hobson (27 September 2011) 'Should Black women oppose the SlutWalk?'.

whether they think a woman is 'asking for it' or not, no matter what she is wearing or how attractive they think she is. A mass-flashing dressed-up like stereotypical 'sluts' accompanied with a 'I'm still not asking for it and I can wear what I want' message, trivialises the brutal mundane reality of rape. Male sexual violence against women has very little to do with the latest fashions, or what women look like.

3.2 The Laughter of Fascists

Watching the whole 12-minute video of the leaked Steubenville rape, where young men joke and laugh about a drugged and unconscious rape victim being dead, is an eerie experience. The video focuses on one male in particular.[62] There is an unnerving way in which the laughing podgy middle-class white boy, who sits with his legs spread apart on a chair, occasionally scratching his crotch, one hand clutching a smart phone that he frequently slaps against his legs, seems innocuous. He is smiling, squirming in his seat with uncontrollable laughter, and having a good time. He looks wholesome, if a little over-fed. His expression seems completely bereft of malice, he looks open, happy, an all-American fun-loving dude. The whole room is full of laughing males. In the face of all this raucous laughter, my failure to laugh, my awareness that my expression was horrified, made me pause, momentarily. I felt the presence of something instructing me to smile and laugh, a subtle 'boys will be boys' message which nudged me to lighten up and indulge their humour. But then I listened to what he and the rest of the males were saying and any possibility of laughter vanished.

This uncanny moment made me realise that the disconnect between someone laughing and smiling and what they are actually saying as they laugh is powerful. And I realised

---

62 See the Steubenville video at: <www.youtube.com/watch?v=W1oahqCzwcY> (accessed 21 July 2013).

that I had experienced this disconnect countless times in the past when men had delivered insults with smiles, had thrown their heads back and laughed at my shocked expression. Hadn't I also learnt how to smile and laugh with them in order to avoid being subjected to overtly violent verbal abuse? There were many times when I had not laughed, when I had called out the abuse for what it was, but most of the times I had done this had led to exhausting arguments. I had often smiled weakly and decided to make an exit, despairing inwardly at how many men pass abuse off as a joke. And also thinking, at times, that a smiling laughing misogynist was better than a screaming and openly violent one. The abusive humour was not, in my experience, the speciality of bad-taste working-class men: I'd heard it from barristers, upper-middle-class journalists, politicians, professors, psychologists, musicians, environmental scientists, and so on. Contemptuous smiles, satirical comments, patronising responses that frame women as laughable idiots, or hysterical psychos, a thousand carefully aimed nasty put-downs said with an ironic smirk and a malicious laugh disguised as healthy good humour.

While the laughter of the all-American dude on the video seems spontaneous at first, it very quickly becomes forced. As soon as I notice this, I also notice that *a rifle is casually lying on the floor behind his chair.* He searches, almost desperately for another joke, another way of describing her death—she is as "dead as O.J. Simpsons' wife," hahaha, she is as "dead as Robert Kennedy," hahaha, "maybe her dying wish was to be raped," hahaha, and so on, and so forth. The man is convulsed with laughter but it would be a mistake to diagnose him as a sociopath, as an exception to the norm, when rape jokes are so common. He has been entitled by a culture that frames sexual assault with canned laughter and which promotes hardcore rape pornography as 'edgy' comedy. He seems to struggle to come up with another punchline, another rape joke. Beneath the hysterical laughter that seems to pour out of him spontaneously, one can glimpse a serious effort to dredge up yet another joke. Occasionally his jokes are not met with laughter and he pauses, struggling for a moment, uncomfortable and a bit worried as his mind searches for another joke, another way of mocking her. She is as dead as … she is as dead as … she is as dead as … It is as though the canned laughter of misogyny has colonised him and now laughs through him: repetitive, mindless, and robotic, despite the corn-fed grin and thigh-slapping.

Each patriarchal nation expresses its hatred of women in culturally specific ways, and in Australia this hatred splattered the first female Prime Minister, Julia Gillard, from 2010 to 2013, with a crude violence which far too many women are familiar with. Aggressive public verbal abuse of women is de rigueur in Australia: a raw, festering hatred of women seems to be simmering beneath the surface, waiting to be triggered at any moment in the hyper-macho racist frontier culture. It seems to be especially bad in Western Australia, where lesbians are spat on in the streets for holding hands, verbally abused and attacked, where eggs are thrown from cars, women are randomly hit, pushed, groped, threatened. The misogynistic aggression and violence is so everyday that one lives with a sense of being continually threatened. It is easier, of course, if one is with a man. And perhaps that is the point of the violence.

Julia Gillard was subjected to a not very subtle homophobic misogyny which repeatedly abused her for not having any children, not being married and having a male partner who is a hairdresser. This was itself enough to make the heads of misogynists explode with righteous heterofascist rage and drove a campaign of abuse, which passed itself off as humour. For example, an especially creepy man named Larry Pickering drew daily sickening cartoons of Gillard: in some she was depicted with enormous strap-on dildos, and in others she had been stabbed (and he emailed these cartoons to all politicians day after day). When Anne Summers named the abuse, he called Summers a "thing."[63] As Summers pointed out, one of the tragedies of the public abuse of Gillard was that women in the Australian Labor Party did not stand together to strongly challenge the abuse of their Prime Minister. She was, in effect, unguarded, unprotected, on her own.[64]

The French aristocrat de Sade is not only the father of contemporary pornography—and a source of the misguided libertarian Left's insistence that pornography is oppositional— but he also laid bare the political function of sadistic laughter. Malice is performed, not only through torture and rape but also psychologically, by laughing at suffering. The more vulnerable the victim, the more enjoyable the sadistic pleasure. The greater the distance between the victim and any protective authority or law, the easier it is to torture her. As Adorno and Horkheimer comment:

> [T]he signs of powerlessness, sudden uncoordinated movements, animal fear, confusion, awaken the thirst for blood ... Domination comes really into its own principle of discipline when the quarry is cornered and desperate. The fear that no longer threatens the dominator himself explodes in hearty laughter (1992, p. 112).

Rape humour signals that rape culture has escaped the law. The laughter is a malicious affirmation of a culture that recognises that, although rape might officially be a crime, the majority of

---

63 See <http://www.abc.net.au/local/stories/2013/06/27/3791203.htm> and <http://pickeringpost.com/article/summers-winter-of-discontent/866> and <http://www.smh.com.au/comment/mad-as-hell-and-not-ready-to-make-nice-20130712-2pv9d.html> (accessed 21 July 2013).

64 Gillard eventually challenged some of the misogyny from the Liberal National Party opposition in a speech which was discussed by the media around the world and which went viral. See <http://www.youtube.com/watch?v=ihd7ofrwQX0>. However, the speech provoked a backlash in Australia and she suffered a fall in popularity and was eventually dumped by the Labor Party in June 2013. See <http://www.theguardian.com/world/2013/jul/26/julia-gillard-misogyny-kevin-rudd> (accessed 15 August 2013).

rapists walk free without even having to endure the discomfort of being accused by victims or publicly or privately shamed.

The two Steubenville rapists will spend at least one year and at least two years respectively in prison. The man who makes endless rape jokes in the video has not been charged. However, Deric Lostutter (a member of Anonymous), who exposed the video to the world, faces ten years in prison. He writes in his blog that 12 armed FBI SWAT agents in full riot gear charged into his house and pointed their M–16 assault rifles at his head, handcuffed him and cleared out his house.[65]

Rape humour signals that the victim-blaming which feminists have fought against for decades has triumphed and that the sexual assault of women is permissible because victims inhabit a culture in which their suffering invites, not compassion, but a predatory, malicious laughter. As Susan Brownmiller writes, "the appeal of the sexual outlaw has always been profound" (1975, p. 299).

---

65 See <http://www.huffingtonpost.com/2013/06/07/deric-lostutter-raid-kyanonymoussteubenville_n_3403000.html> (accessed 21st July 2013).

4.0 *Arbeit macht frei*: Sexing Austerity

> Here the struggle to survive is without respite, because everyone is desperately and ferociously alone.
>
> —Primo Levi, *If This Is a Man* (2011, p. 49)

'Work brings freedom': *Arbeit macht frei.* The sign that still hangs over the entrance of Auschwitz[66] may as well be the ironic motto for austerity. In the name of the global financial crisis, patriarchal capitalism is rapidly transforming into austerity fascism. Sharply rising unemployment; unaffordable housing, food, electricity and gas; the ruthless destruction of the remains of the welfare state; higher consumption taxes; increasingly malicious policies designed to humiliate and punish the vulnerable; the normalisation of casual, part-time, low-wage, short-term contract work; a mass reduction in wages; the corporate and military surveillance of civilian populations; the elimination of international human rights by democratic governments; cuts to public service jobs, education and health; the reduction of pension schemes; higher retirement ages; growing student debt; the criminalisation of protests; cuts to legal aid; the rise of openly fascist parties; intensified state-sanctioned xenophobia; demonising of asylum seekers; racist murders and attacks; and

---

66 For a photograph of the sign see <http://fcit.usf.edu/holocaust/GALL31R/00001.htm> (accessed 31 August 2013).

increased police brutality, are all escalating *indefinitely*. Some say there is a revolution in process and there are sporadic anti-austerity marches across the world—sometimes involving millions and leading to violent clashes with riot police—coordinated strikes, as well as spectacular protests such as the Occupy Movement. However, the *real* revolution is by the ruling corporate patriarchal global elite who are enforcing radical forms of oppression without effective opposition.

Many in the Left have called this a class war, and while it clearly is, it is also a sex war. Women and their children, always the poorest of the poor, have come under a calculated, often invisibilised, attack by austerity fascism. In an era in which the criminal global patriarchal corporate elite is destroying millions of women's lives, mainstreamed hip feminist pornified protests such as SlutWalk seem like diversionary spectacles. Indeed, the tragedy (if it could be dignified as such) of mainstream western feminism is the pervasive betrayal of poor women, and most brutally, single mothers.

Evidence is emerging that austerity is creating a gendered restructuring of the workplace. More women than men are losing jobs. According to the UK National Organisation of Statistics (NOS), men's unemployment fell in the UK during the start of 2013 by 15,000, while women's unemployment has increased by 40,000.[67] Cuts to welfare also impact on women far more than men. In a 2013 report issued by the Fawcett Society, 'The changing labour market: Delivering for women, delivering for growth', the following was found:

---

67 "Women's unemployment has risen to a 26-year high whilst men's is decreasing … [T]he latest ONS figures (published in April 2013, reflecting February 2013 levels of employment) show women's unemployment now stands at 1.12 million. Overall since the start of 2013, men's unemployment has fallen by 15,000 and women's has increased by 40,000" <http://www.fawcettsociety. org.uk/new-report-warns-of-female-unfriendly-labourmarket-as-womens-unemployment> (accessed 12 September 2013).

Women's unemployment has risen to a 26-year high whilst men's is decreasing;

Government's plans for growth are leaving women behind;

60 per cent of 'new' private sector jobs have gone to men;

Almost three times as many women as men have become 'long term' unemployed in the last two and a half years—103,000 women in comparison to 37,000 men;

Women have borne the brunt of cuts to the public sector workforce so far, and some 75 per cent of these are yet to come;

If the current pattern of women making up the majority of those losing their jobs but the minority of those benefitting from new employment opportunities continues, the worst case scenario would see some 1.48 million women unemployed by 2018;

Failure to take action risks creating a 'female unfriendly' labour market characterised by persistent and rising levels of women's unemployment;

Diminishing pay levels for women, and a widening of the gender pay gap.[68]

The re-masculinisation of the state that began with neo-liberal welfare reforms in the 1990s is now transforming into the re-masculinisation of employment. Not only are women increasingly pushed into degrading low-paid casual work, but they are also increasingly pushed out of work altogether. Women continue to be the underclass, the global Lumpenproletariat. In a 2010 essay in *The New Left Review*, Michael Denning uses the term 'wageless life' to describe the life of the unemployed. Denning begins his essay with the timely statement that today under capitalism "the only thing worse than being exploited is not being exploited." Work is, more than ever, a feminist issue. As unemployment threatens an increasing number of women, exploitation has become preferable.

---

68   <http://www.fawcettsociety.org.uk/new-report-warns-of-female-unfriendly-labour-market-as-womens-unemployment-continues-to-rise/#sthash.x5O97J5G.dpuf> (accessed 13 June 2013).

The western targeting of single mothers by the new austerity fascism, far from being a marginal attack and a 'side-effect' of the necropolitics of patriarchal capitalism, is a *central* political strategy which has been evolved over the last few decades under the self-empowerment banner of neo-liberalism. Recent history shows us that the destruction of welfare protection and the creation of precarious degrading employment almost invariably begin with the targeting of single mothers. 'Work', after all, 'brings freedom', and single mothers who are not in paid work must be liberated by the work camp of corporate patriarchy. For these women, Thatcher's infamous statement, "there is no such thing as society," may as well have meant there is no such thing as feminism.[69]

Single mothers (and their children) are the canaries in the mineshaft of neo-liberalism, yet although attacks against single mothers began decades ago, few recognised the implications of these warnings. Indeed, the corporate embrace of an upwardly mobile, politely non-combative, white middle-class liberal version of feminism has resulted in a broad neglect of the socio-economic oppression of single mothers and poor women in general. The focus on leadership programs for female CEOs, representative equality, and so on, are *liberal* feminist concerns which have little meaning for those who struggle to survive on dwindling benefits and are forced to compete for low-paying dead-end casual jobs in shadowy realms where there is no real protection from workplace sexual harassment, let alone union rights, maternity leave, sick leave, holiday pay, superannuation or pension schemes. Quite simply: an alliance between liberal feminism and capitalism has thrown several generations of women to the patriarchal vampires of the deregulated neo-liberal market place.

---

69 For the 1987 transcript of the interview by *Woman's Own* in which Thatcher said, "There is no such thing as society," see <http://www.margaretthatcher.org/document/106689> (accessed 10 September 2013).

The public socio-economic flogging of single mothers also sends out a powerful warning to all women—it is permissible to oppress single mothers in ways that make a mockery of women's rights. Therefore, all women must avoid slipping down to the level of single mothers if they are to retain a semblance of financial autonomy and have a decent chance at survival. Ironically, however, this 'autonomy' is little more than obedience to the system. But if the 'choice' is between being a respectable wage slave with the hope of increased wages, and being an unpaid or radically underpaid stigmatised slave with little to no chance of ever escaping the 'poverty trap'—and what is cruellest, watching one's/their/our/your children's lives be smashed apart—then most women will do whatever it takes to avoid becoming or staying single mothers. In this way, the flogging of single mothers operates as a form of patriarchal social engineering, as a way of disciplining and controlling not only women who are married to, or living with, their children's fathers, but younger women who are trying to negotiate entering or staying in an increasingly precarious workplace that is still geared toward childless women. Many young women recognise that the situation is a set-up, and know that if they wish to have children they must either have enough earning power to support themselves and their children (which often means being able to afford the outsourcing of their mothering), or find a partner who will support them when they are mothers. It is a situation designed to enforce women's obedience in the public and private sphere. Making the 'right choice' in work and love is now, more than ever, a matter of raw survival. In an environment of harsh austerity, the options for rebellion are narrowing and the 'right choice' is rapidly becoming Far Right. It is possible that a barely concealed terror about the possibility of falling into the gutter zone of single mother scum and becoming a member of the western equivalent of the untouchable caste, is the unacknowledged subtext of a lack of substantive coordinated resistance to austerity fascism by the mainstream women's liberation movement.

Now more than ever, the women's liberation movement needs to confront the violent symbolic and socio-economic warnings that radiate from the oppressed figure of the single mother. Until the political persecution of single mothers is placed at the centre of feminist activism and thinking, and the connections between work, poverty and mothering are thought through in relation to single mothers, the violent tactics of corporate necropolitics will continue to transform the planet into a fascist work camp where those who are not chosen for exploitation are seen as expendable human waste. Paulo Freire's motto 'learn from below' is increasingly urgent in a world in which many women are now either those who are already below or those who are about to fall.

4.1 *Vernichtung durch Arbeit*: Annihilation through Work

Hester Eisenstein's *Feminism Seduced: How Global Elites Use Women's Labor and Ideas to Exploit the World* (2009) is a tightly argued and devastating tracking of the opportunistic exploitation of the U.S. women's liberation movement by the global corporate patriarchal elite and their puppet governments. Eisenstein's analysis of the neutralisation of class-consciousness within feminism resonates with my own experience and the lives of many women I know who feel betrayed and insulted by liberal feminism, especially single mothers who are being driven into the ground with the impossible demand to earn a wage while mothering their young children. Women have to juggle inflexible work hours with the end of the school day and school holidays, shopping, cooking, housework, homework, bills, illness, broken appliances and cars, hostile landlords and real estate agents, punishing employers, an escalating cost of living, a family court, child support agency and social security system which is overtly contemptuous, while trying to ward off and negotiate an incessant social disgust directed at them because they are not living with a man.

The women I know are single mothers because they had been abandoned by the fathers of their children or had escaped domestic violence; none have chosen poverty, it has been forced on them by men, and then patriarchy has punished them for being abandoned and abused by men. All speak of the shock they experienced when they were re-abandoned by women in their community who, more often than not, immediately sided with the very men who had beaten, exploited and abandoned them. "Single mothers are seen as scum," one self-employed Australian single mother tells me. Another single mother says, in a matter-of-fact kind of way, that "a woman without a man has no value."

In a desperate attempt to ward off community hate, 'Alice' sacrifices the basics, like proper heating and healthy food, to make sure that she and her three children are well dressed. Her former husband abandoned her and their children after years of verbal abuse, telling her and their friends that he just wasn't cut out to be a father. Although he only sees his children once a fortnight, he refuses to allow Alice to return to her mother who lives in another country. Exiled from any family support, continually exhausted and depressed from the stress of working and caring for her children and living in precarious rental accommodation, she tells me that she often wishes she was dead. A lover lived with her for almost a year but contributed a minimal amount of money and food, even though his salary was six times the size of hers. She told me it was like having an extra child to look after, but a child that was jealous of her actual children. After he left her, the network of mothers and fathers she had spent almost two years being friends with abruptly shunned her.

'Anna', having left her husband after years of verbal and physical violence (which escalated while she was pregnant and left her partially blind) then had to witness her still abusive ex-husband dragging her crying two-year-old from her every week. Her son would wrap his arms around her neck and refuse to let go. Her ex-husband would take her crying son from her and leave him in a day-care centre in accordance with 'shared parenting' court orders that were forced on her while she was on welfare and without adequate legal representation.[70] For the first year of the forced weekly removal of her child she would curl up in a foetal position on the floor afterwards, and put her hands over her ears to try and block out the memory of her son crying "No, no, I want mummy." Anna tried to visit her son at his day-care centre on the day of his fourth birthday but was told by the female manager that she was not allowed to see him because court orders stated that he was in the care of her husband during that part of the week. As the legal scholar Carol Smart (2001) has shown, institutionalised prejudice against single mothers in the court system continues to ruin the lives of single mothers and their children, legitimising a barbaric contempt for vulnerable women and children.[71]

Where is feminism in the sneers, smirks and turned backs of partnered and married women at the school drop-off and pick-up? What kind of equality, humanity and support is offered to vulnerable women and their children by the unchallenged normative contempt of men who have been trained to think of single mothers as 'damaged goods' or 'sluts' who deserve to be exploited and abused, in the unnamed workplace discrimination, in the all too frequently female representative of the government agencies (child support, social security) that routinely patronise, ignore, misinform, put on hold and fail to call back single mothers?

---

70 Disgustingly, men are often more violent towards women during pregnancy. That pregnant women are beaten by their partners is one of the more horrifying symptoms of misogyny. See, for example, <http://www.womensaid. ie/campaigns/domesticviolenc1.html> (accessed 15 August 2013).

71 See also Petrie and Griffin (2011).

Following on from historian Nancy McLean (2002), Eisenstein argues that the abolition of the 'family wage' has transformed women's lives far more than second wave feminism (2009, p. 107). The family wage (or breadwinner wage) was the achievement of working-class struggles in the nineteenth and early twentieth centuries (Brenner, 2000, pp. 11–58) and, importantly, a wage that recognised that mothers and children needed financial support to survive, and that being a mother is work. "In the low-wage economy that replaced it, no such concept remained" (Eisenstein, 2009, p. 117). In short, the destruction of the family wage and the pushing of mothers into the workforce, mostly into the expanding service sector, operated to keep wages down. Championing the destruction of the family wage because it was argued to entrench the breadwinner–housewife model which supported the sexual division of labour and women's enslavement in the domestic sphere, liberal feminism idealised paid work as the key to women's liberation. Talking about the U.S.A., Eisenstein points out that

> the idea that all women should work played right into the hands of those seeking welfare reform. The idea that women ought to be working for wages reinforced the argument against paying for 'welfare queens'. Thus, a pillar of the New Deal was toppled with the aid of the ideology of feminism … As women with education and access climbed the corporate ladder, reaching near parity with male middle managers, uneducated, poor women crowded into the jobs offered by retail organizations such as Wal-Mart, where much of the workforce was able to subsist only with the aid of food vouchers, Medicaid, and section 8 housing. As poverty steadily increased under the George W. Bush administration, a new class divide opened up between the women for whom feminism was a ticket to advancement, and those left behind in the growing pool of the working poor—including new immigrants and those cut off from welfare (2009, p. 107).

As many know, because it is impossible to raise a family on a single middle-class (let alone a working-class) wage, mothers must work when their children are still babies. This does not apply, of course, to the upper-middle-classes or those with inherited wealth, but it does apply to an increasing majority of mothers. The growth of the heavily exploitative secondary labour market, of low-paid, part-time, casual, dead-end work, was largely built on the backs of women, many of whom were mothers. Significantly, the abolition of the family wage did not overcome the sexual division of labour, as liberal feminists had imagined it would. The double-shift, working inside and outside the home, is more like an endless hell than a golden nirvana of self-empowered financial autonomy. Now women worked inside and outside the home, often cleaning toilets, cooking and serving food, taking care of wealthier women's children, and then turned around to go home and clean toilets, cook and serve food and take care of their own children. The new anguish was that women were being forced to sacrifice time with their children so that their children could survive. Often, the largest portion of the wages that working women earn are given to for-profit agencies which care for their children in day care, after-school care, holiday care, and so on it goes. Day care from 8 am to 6 pm, five-days-a-week for three-month-old children is not uncommon for those who can, or must, afford it. Patriarchal capitalism is a child-hating mother-hating system which values work that contributes to the destruction and exploitation of life over and above work which nurtures life.

Once the family wage had been destroyed and corporate patriarchy had cannibalised women's bodies and minds with degrading low-paid work, the welfare system was dismantled. These attacks meant, effectively, that women had to become even more obedient to men in the home, and to their capitalist employers, if they wished to avoid dangerous levels of abject poverty for themselves and their children. As Eisenstein comments:

> [T]he widespread acceptance of waged work for women did not go unnoticed by policy makers. The idea that women should be in the paid labor force was so hegemonic in the 1990s that the welfare "reform" legislation of 1996, the Personal Responsibility and Work Opportunity Reconciliation Act (PRWORA), made this its centerpiece. Carrying out a key element in the neoliberal agenda of undoing the social policies of the New Deal, welfare reform devolved responsibility to the states, removed the idea of welfare as an entitlement to pay a poor single mother needing assistance with taking care of her children, and, most importunately, instituted *workfare* as a requirement. Single mothers would no longer have the safety net of a government subsidy, no matter how inadequate, in exchange for raising their children (2009, p. 123, my emphasis).

Poor single mothers were expected to look after themselves without state support. The welfare reforms were an act of civil war against poor women and the battle cry was made in the name of class and race hate. It was a "meat axe for people to swing at what already was a shredded safety net" (Pierce, 2012) As Charles Pierce writes, the welfare reforms were sold with "fairy tales about young bucks buying steaks and welfare queens with their Cadillacs … when it actually gave everybody permission not to care about poverty anymore" (Pierce, 2012).[72] If one was poor, one had no one to blame but oneself, and women, already blamed for domestic violence and rape, could easily be blamed for being destitute.

The welfare reforms that earlier feminists had fought for and achieved between 1910 and 1920 were destroyed in the name of liberal feminism in the mid-1990s (Gordon, 1994, p. 37; Eisenstein, 2009, p. 123). Although the "white women's reform community of approximately 1890–1935" (Gordon,

---

72 See <http://theweek.com/article/index/226565/did-bill-clintons-welfare-reforms-make-the-great-recessionworse> (accessed 17 August 2013).

1994, p. 55) was corrupted by race and class prejudices, they did secure the right of mothers to have access to minimal welfare (Gordon, 1994, p. 284). The basis of their argument was the recognition that mothering children should be respected as important unpaid labour (Snyder, 2005, p. 12). Yet as Eisenstein points out, mainstream feminist organisations in the 1990s viewed this argument as supporting traditional patriarchal values. The majority of members of the National Organization of Women (NOW) were reluctant to resist the 'end of welfare as we know it' reforms. Their president Jill Ireland, however, attempted to mobilise against the reforms by seeking an alliance with the National Welfare Rights Union 'Up and Out of Poverty Now!' campaign. NOW marched, some women went on hunger strikes, and attempted to block the new legislation. They failed. Some argue it was because NOW's attempts were too late, and that the consciousness of its mainly middle-class members was still infected with unreconstructed prejudice towards poor women. Gwendolyn Mink comments that a dominant white middle-class feminism which "calibrated independence in terms of labour market attachment, and that equated equality with fertility control, not with the right to have or care for children," lay beneath an implicit support for the destruction of welfare for single mothers (Mink, 2001, p. 7). Mink, a welfare feminist activist and scholar, stated that effort was needed to combat "the racism and solipsism that lured some feminists into the war against poor women" (Mink, 2001, p. 7).

After several decades of neo-liberalism, class inequality between women has become entrenched and single mothers are still being punished. As Eisenstein writes, "perhaps the most dramatic unintended impact of feminist activism has been the emergence of a serious class divide among women" (2009, p. 130). Today that divide is deepening. She also asks: "[I]s it hyperbole to speak of a marriage made in heaven between corporations and the mainstream women's movement?"

(2009, p. 132). The branding of feminism as girl power, and the ideological consensus between neo-liberal corporate patriarchy and mainstream feminist 'self-empowerment' and 'self-responsibility' doctrines would suggest that it *is* a happy marriage. But for those who have left marriages, partnerships, or decided to keep a child after a brief fling, this marriage is a living hell. Into the symbolic rubbish bin of 'single mother' are thrown immigrants, indigenous women, teenagers, black women, poor ethnic minorities, women who have fled sexually, physically, psychologically and economically abusive men, women who have been abandoned by partners and families. Of course there is a small minority of single mothers who have former male partners who give them houses, and enough child support to keep them from poverty, but they are in the minority and are all too often the straw women of the lunatic fringe men's rights movement who bellow about the persecution of single fathers by single mothers via the family court and child support agencies. The reality for most single mothers is more like this:

> It's all the stresses in the world ... You know what I'm saying. You have to do all these things, and then you have to worry about child care, making it home in time to feed them, put them in the tub, clean up the house ... You're trying to do all this on your own, with no help. What's the word for it? I don't even know the word for it? (Delia Carter cited in Collins and Mayer, 2010, p. 10).

Eisenstein's argument has been made elsewhere by numerous socialist feminist activists and theorists. She is clear that she is not supporting a return to the family wage–male breadwinner–housewife model but rather that she wants increased wages for poor women and a humane welfare system. By recognising that mothering is a form of human labour that is the foundation of human life and should be respected as such, Hester Eisenstein has more in common with Johnnie Tillmon (mother of six, a Los Angeles laundrywoman, and a national welfare rights leader), than she does with the U.S. Christian right-wing 'angel in the house' tea party people who have shot to prominence in recent years. Tillmon said in 1972: "[S]tart paying women a living wage for doing work we are already doing—child raising and housekeeping. And the welfare crisis would be over. Just like that."[73]

Feminists have rightly suggested introducing a Universal Basic Income (UBI) which protects women from economic violence and such ideas are now urgently important (Hyman, 1999; Hawthorne, 2002). "What if," asks Eisenstein,

> ... the leadership of the women's movements had focused, not on gaining access to top levels of professional work—law, medicine, politics—but on addressing the economic needs of the poorest women? ... [A]s Heather Booth notes, one of the mistakes of the feminist movement as a whole was that 'we aimed at the top', rather than at the bottom, where the poorest women were, and are (2009, p. 132).

It is also important to note that feminist attempts at protecting poor women have been marginalised by a dominant liberal feminist invisibilisation of class. In an era in which austerity is pushing more women into poverty, it is more important than ever that feminism not only addresses the needs of the poorest women, but that feminists break their silence about their own class oppression and refuse to be shamed for not conforming to the neo-liberal corporate-sponsored advertisement of what a 'tasteful feminist' is meant to be.

4.2 *Jaden das Seine:* Everyone Gets What She Deserves

It is uncanny how perfectly so many of the Nazi death camp slogans fit the current patriarchal ideology of neo-liberal austerity fascism. The slogan *Jaden das Seine,* which literally

---

73 <www.albany.edu/faculty/cb598342/tillmon.doc> (accessed 22 June 2013).

means 'to each his own' or 'everyone gets what he deserves', was used in the notorious Buchenwald camp. The slogan neatly encapsulates the ideology of neo-liberal marketplace psychology that promotes the selfishness of 'looking out for number one' in order to discredit acts of human solidarity as self-destructive weakness. Those who do not know how to take care of themselves have only themselves to blame: they are 'losers' in the game of life, to be despised and shunned. Victims are human waste. "The flip side of 'Don't be a victim' is 'Don't rescue' any other victims" (Ehrenreich and English, 1989, p. 303). Or, as a high-ranking white upper-middle-class member of the Australian Labor Party once advised me, if someone is drowning, kick them away before they drag you down with them. The callous hegemonic neo-liberal common sense of 'save yourself because no one else will' or 'no one can save anyone else' is a distant echo of the ethos of the death camps which Primo Levi explored so honestly in his work. Avoid contact with victims unless they can meet your needs. When they no longer meet your needs, move on. One must take care of one's own needs first. "The *needs* have an inherent legitimacy—the *people* are replaceable" (Ehrenreich and English, 1989, p. 304).

One must compete for survival in the camps as though one's fate has nothing to do with the structure of the camp itself, or the fact that one is trapped in a camp, but rather how well and how long one can survive. As Levi writes, "the Lager was pre-eminently a gigantic biological and social experiment" (2011, p. 93). Most of the women and children were immediately sent to the gas chambers, their dead bodies plundered and incinerated. Women and children were not considered to be economically viable workers. Although everyone in the camps were thought of as human vermin, only those who were fit for exploitation were allowed to live for as long as they could work. Denning's observation about life under capitalism today, that 'the only thing worse than being exploited is not being exploited', is chilling because it hints that the fate of those who are not 'fit' for exploitation is—yet again—a deadly form of symbolic and material degradation.

Single mothers, as Anna Marie Smith observes, are now routinely described as lives unworthy of being lived.

> There is hardly any difference between the slurs that are commonly circulated in American society and government about the welfare mother—that is, the demonizing representations that construct her as a species of vermin or pestilence—and the absolutely obnoxious and horrific claims that her life is not worth living and does not deserve to be lived (2010).

To a poor white single mother in a twenty-first century western democracy, trying to take care of her children in the face of institutionalised discrimination, are flung words from the white male intelligentsia, such as "die screaming in hell," "do us all a favour and kill yourself," "shut up and go play in traffic." Less flamboyant expressions of revulsion are familiar to many single mothers: from the intrusive and contemptuous private and public policing of their homes, appearance, their children, sanity, their occupations, social status and background, to levels of social shunning which effectively expel them from the community. The mass emotional abuse of single mothers is one of the hidden injuries of patriarchal capitalism. There are many forms of recognised emotional abuse. Overt aggression is just one form. Indirect emotional abuse passes as patronising, belittling and minimising, in short, treating someone as though they are subnormal or inferior. Then there are the many forms of denying someone's actual material and emotional reality by, for example, abusing someone and then pretending it hasn't happened. It is usually called 'gaslighting', and is a recognised way of driving someone out of their mind by perpetually invalidating their own perception of reality. There is also the technique of withholding, or just denying, someone's humanity to the extent that one pretends they do not exist: refusing to reply, communicate, giving someone the 'silent treatment'. As Smith (2010) argues in her analysis of the neo-eugenicist hatred of single mothers, the emotional abuse is uttered within the context of the system's relentless oppression of single mothers.

One of the pervasive stereotypes of single mothers—one of the more pernicious victim-blaming ones—is that single mothers make 'bad choices' in relationships and all too often expose their children to abuse and neglect by staggering from one abusive man to the next. The mainstream patriarchal media routinely feature sensational victim-blaming stories about the abuse of single mothers and their children by men.[74] But once all of this is put into the context of a single-mother-hating culture, it is more probable that single mothers are targeted by men, not only because it is permissible to punish socially and economically vulnerable women with children, but because the abuse of single mothers is a central strategy in the oppression of all women.

One is tempted to paraphrase Susan Brownmiller's statement about rape culture and write that a world in which single mothers and their children were not persecuted would be a world in which women could work and mother without fear. That single mothers and their children are persecuted provides a sufficient threat to keep all mothers and potential mothers in a constant state of intimidation, forever conscious of the knowledge that patriarchy will turn on them at any time with a swiftness born of harmful intent. Rather than society's deviants, men who oppress single mothers and their children serve, in effect, as frontline masculine shock troops, terrorist guerrillas in a long battle over the control of women's ability to give birth to, and care for, human beings.

---

74 See the account of a 'single mother' who was 'seduced' by Jon Venables, one of James Bulger's murderers: <http://goo.gl/M2NA4s>, and of course the infer-ence that her willingness to be seduced put her own toddler at risk. "She nearly let him see her son" <http://goo.gl/VydwXW> (accessed 17 August 2013).

The history of patriarchal persecution of single mothers
is long and barbaric, even leaving aside the mass murder of
single mothers as witches several hundred years ago. The Poor
Law Act (1838) meant that single mothers and their children
had to live in workhouses, which were little more than abusive
and heavily exploitative work camps. During the late Victorian
era single mothers were placed in the workhouse while their
children were handed over for adoption to wet nurses in 'baby
farms', often to be slowly starved to death, their corpses tossed
into the Thames or buried in gardens (Arnot, 1994). There is
the train wreck of dehumanising laws that prevented married
women from working without their husbands' permission, that
sacked women if they got married, and punished mothers who
left marriages, which were only challenged in the 1970s and
1980s. The removal and forced adoption of newborn babies
from significant numbers of white single unmarried mothers
that occurred up until 1982 in Australia has only recently (after
decades of activism) received a government apology.[75] But
saying 'sorry' is an archly neo-liberal tactic; symbolic concern
replaces restitution, as though the thousands of broken women
and children should now feel deep gratitude for the apology
of a government. Unmarried mothers or mothers without
husbands have long been punished.

Sadly, dramatic cuts to single parenting payments, or
'single mother pensions', were enforced on 1 January 2013 in
Australia:

> Under the changes, sole parents will be placed on the Newstart dole
> once their youngest child turns 8. This amounts to an average loss of
> $140 in weekly income and in some cases up to $200. Newstart pays
> just $246 a week, or $35 a day for a single adult. According to the

75 Julia Gillard, the first female Prime Minister of Australia, had enough compassion
and integrity to recognise and apologise to the women and children who
had been harmed by forced adoption. See <http://www.ag.gov.au/About/
ForcedAdoptionsApology/Pages/default.aspx> (accessed 15 August 2013).

Australian Council of Social Services (ACOSS), this figure is $100 beneath the poverty line. Previously, single parents lost the support pension when their youngest child turned 16 (Church, 2013).[76]

For many single mothers this results in not being able to afford heating during winter, clothes and food, let alone paying the rent or the mortgage, plus having their credit rating destroyed. Such conditions also mean that women in relationships with abusive men will find it increasingly difficult to leave, which in turn means that their children will be at risk from domestic violence and worse.

In 2011 London convulsed with anger after police shot Mark Duggan, a poor Anglo-African. David Cameron, leader of the conservative party, announced that 'fatherless children' were to blame for the street violence.[77] An already deeply ingrained prejudice against poor single mothers erupted. In an insightful article on the ways in which the British press blamed the 2011 London riots on single mothers, Tanya Gold (2011) writes:

> [W]hat we have today is slightly better, but of the same vindictive hue … I do not know why single mothers are singled out for judgment by the rest. I suspect it is, in the end, the remnants of an ancient misogyny, damning women for failing in that most basic role— making men happy—and seeking independence for themselves. A sane government would provide cheap childcare, of course, and force companies to offer jobs with flexible working hours. But they are not in the business of solutions. They want punishment.

---

76 However, in 2010 Gillard did seek to expand family law definitions of domestic violence in order to protect children. See <http://www.thefamilylawdirectory.com. au/article/safety-first-in-gillards-family-lawchanges.html> (accessed 16 August 2013). And for background on the impact of the family courts on children see <http://www.theage.com.au/national/the-kids-are-not-all-right-20110816-1iw7l.html> (accessed 15 August 2013).

77 For the speech Cameron made about the riots see <http://www.theguardian.com/politics/blog/2011/aug/15/england-riots-cameron-miliband-speeches> (accessed 15 August 2013).

Single mothers don't know how to make men happy which is why men have abused and/or abandoned them and why they have 'problems' with other men, or so it goes. The punishment of single mothers for failing to make men happy is a very troubling indication that our culture is very far from civilised, democratic, rational, humane or enlightened. Liberty! Equality! Fraternity! And for women, be pleasing to men or we will cut you off from society, grind your life into the gutter and humiliate you! And your children!

To return to the words of the poor single mother quoted earlier: "You're trying to do all this on your own, with no help. *What's the word for it? I don't even know the word for it*" (my emphasis). We could reply to her that the name she is searching for is 'patriarchal capitalism', 'austerity' or 'neo-liberalism' and explain to her that her experience of exploitation is a product of these political systems. But it is very likely that she already knows all about male domination and class oppression, neo-liberal welfare reforms and austerity because their lessons have smashed up her life. Instead of assuming that we know the answer to her question "What's the word for it?" and so, potentially, the solution to her suffering, what if her question becomes our question? If 'the problem that had no name' was Betty Friedan's (1963/1983) description of the anguish of the lonely 1950s housewife, what do we call the intensified social exclusion and exploitation of the single mother of 2013? It is possible that, in an era of rapidly expanding austerity fascism, we do not as yet have the political and conceptual tools to name and comprehend the force that is breaking her life and millions of other women's lives without any substantial opposition from the Left or the mainstream women's movement.

What it looks and feels like is the triumph of a new form of patriarchal fascism that is evolving and spreading so quickly that one cannot quite see the edges of what it will become or what it is already. There is a connection between the almost daily mainstream media reports about the billions of unpaid taxes of global corporations which invoke an outrage (which too often becomes a quiet defeatism) and a return to the more immediate issue of personal survival; and the stories about mass demonstrations which invoke a brief hope … but which too often turns into a quiet despair, when not only does nothing change, but the screws are tightened the very next day. I watch the distant protests of the so-called third world proletarian women and it strikes me that *they are not afraid to hate their oppressors and they are not alone in their anger.*

But in the west, is this single mothers' endless atomised exploitation the product of a form of control that is in the process of being enforced in the rebellious nations? Is the single mother's exploited loneliness a kind of incomprehensible subaltern language, or is her radical abandonment unnameable because it is forbidden to name this isolating exploitation as a political tactic in women's oppression? The social shunning of single mothers is political even while it often occurs without any overt acts of violence: phone calls that are not returned, invitations which are never given, turned backs, lowered voices, sniffs, titters, nasty glances, the repetitive rituals of exclusion, a thousand little micro-fascisms, a thousand little exterminations. But most of all: silence. Her emotional life is denied, her dreams, passions, history, her humanity, becomes unspeakable. *Because no one is interested.* The petty petit bourgeois symbolic murder of single mothers must be performed with the appearance of refinement: one does not punch 'the other' in the stomach, one merely calmly observes, generously corrects and informs, and then shuns. One must hide one's hate with a polite smile or an averted gaze. It is only permissible to speak to the wretched of the earth if it leads to social or financial gain, and single mothers are very far from value-adding. Caught between the incessant bureaucratic insults of the system (social security, family courts, child support, doctors, corporations, banks, work, housing) and a contemptuous silence, she lives unguarded in the community;

there is nothing which stands between her and the murderous function of the state.

Stephanie Bottrill was a 53-year-old single mother who brought up two children in Birmingham. She was too poor to heat her home during winter, could not afford to eat, and faced the loss of her home of 18 years because of the 'bedroom tax'. Before she killed herself in May 2013 by walking into a truck, she told her neighbours: "*I can't afford to live anymore*" (Varma, 13 May 2013).[78] In a suicide letter to her son she blamed the government for her death. In another incident, a middle-aged single mother standing on the edge of the fifth floor of a car park in Birmingham shouts about the government, child support and her house, before leaping 100 feet (30 metres) to her death in front of a large crowd (Lillington, 18 June 2013). Commenting on the newspaper article (via *Birmingham Mail* website) a woman writes: "[W]e in plymouth [*sic*] also had a woman jump off the top floor of one of our car parks last week just *what is going on I don't know …*" (my emphasis). Most of the comments on the newspaper articles about these single mother suicides argue that the government has killed them. Many also express awareness that a form of fascism has taken control: "I [*sic*] surprised they don't just open up gas chambers in middle of cities"; "The more people they drive to suicide the less they have to pay out and the more they can massage figures"; "They deserve to be charged with genocide against the people." And then, amongst the anger at the government's indirect killing of single mothers, there is the bark of the new fascism—harsh, cold, irrational, and ruthlessly misogynistic:

> The privileged sex thinks that she is entitled to every comfort of life just because she has a vagina … and when theirs [*sic*] entitlements are not met they feel angry. They must learn that they are entitled to those things only that they earn.

---

78 See also <http://johnnyvoid.wordpress.com/2013/05/11/this-is-what-austerity-looks-like-first-suicide-due-tobedroom-tax-reported/> (accessed 12 July 2013).

This fascism is at the heart of the cruel shunning that leads to the murderous abandonment of single mothers by society. Replying to the fascist, a single mother writes:

> The people who think this lady is selfish has [sic] obviously never been on the depressed level she has and struggled with money like she has (I'm there now). Bringing up kids with no money and not being able to afford to feed them or give them little luxuries is part of the depression, feeling useless and guilty, she obviously thought they would be better off without her ...[79]

Single mothers are expected to feel guilt not anger, to feel shame not indignation. Any other emotional response to their oppression is criminalised and pathologised. Did these single mothers kill themselves because they decided, after thinking it through, that their children would be better off with a dead mother than a mother who was considered to be human vermin? Is the hatred of single mothers so intense that mothers are killing themselves rather than contaminating their children socially: have they weighed up the taboo against suicide, and the grief it will cause, against the stigma of being seen as sub-human, and decided that their children are 'better off' without them? What does it mean when a single mother in a western democracy states: "*I can't afford to live anymore*" and kills herself by walking into a truck?

> Fascism, like desire is scattered everywhere in separate bits and pieces, within the whole social realm; it crystallises in one place or another, depending on the relationship of force. It can be said of fascism that it is all-powerful and, at the same time, ridiculously weak. And whether it is the former or the latter depends on the capacity of collective arrangements, subject-groups, to connect the social libido, on every level, with the whole range of revolutionary machines of desire (Guattari, 2009a, p. 171).

---

79 See comments on this story <http://www.birminghammail.co.uk/news/local-news/solihull-suicide-tragedy-gran-spent-3660813> (accessed 12 July 2013).

Patriarchal fascism crystallises in the lives of single mothers who commit suicide and is solidifying in the lives of the submerged, the fallen, unemployed and heavily exploited, just as it is poisoning the whole social realm. There are various excuses made for the new barbarism, most of which are economic, but actions, as they say, speak louder than words, and it is clear that the violently irrational force of the new world order is shooting down life with a re-loaded misogyny.

5.0 Another World Is Possible: Reversing Barbarism

The political imagination of contemporary feminism is at a standstill … If feminism takes this opportunity to shake off its current imperialist and consumerist sheen it would once again place its vital transformative political demands centre-stage, and shuffle off its current one-dimensionality for good.

—Nina Power, *One Dimensional Woman* (2009, p. 69)

Marillyn Hewson grew up in America during second wave feminism; she has a Bachelor of Science, a Master of Arts in economics from the University of Alabama and completed the Harvard Business School executive development programme. In 2010, 2011 and 2012 *Forbes* magazine listed her as one of the most powerful women in business. She is the CEO of a private corporation that secured $36 billion from the United States government in 2008, the largest amount of cash to a single corporation from any government in history. Her corporation is Lockheed Martin, the most successful arms manufacturing corporation on the planet.[80] Hewson is *kick ass*; she has achieved

---

80 For information on Lockheed Martin see <http://www.lockheedmartin.com> (accessed 25 August 2013). See also Amina Mama (28 November 2012):

> US military spending has reached an all-time high, with Iraq, Afghanistan, Pakistan alone costing between $2.2–2.8 trillion so far. Most of this money has been borrowed, contributing significantly to the US's larger-than-ever

formidable success in the male-dominated arms industry. But this is, surely, nothing to celebrate.

The Stockholm International Peace Research Institute (SIPRI) report on trends in the arms industry in 2011 claims that 44 American arms corporations produce 60% of the total arms sales in the world.[81] They sell to whoever has the money to buy their weapons. Official United States military expenditure has also long constituted roughly half of the world's military spending. Make no mistake, the 'land of the free' is a militarised culture. According to the National War Tax Resistance Coordinating Committee (NWTRCC), 47% of the 2014 United States budget is devoted to military expenses.[82] It is very probable that the actual amount is much larger, as the military industrial complex has a history of hiding their budget expenses under other names such as 'foreign aid'.

---

debt burden, and the US financial crisis. While the recession has taken its toll, military contractors have profited from significantly more public money, amounting to over 400 billion received in contracts in 2008, the highest level since World War II.

'Where we must stand: African women in an age of war' <http://www.opendemocracy.net/5050/amina-mama/where-we-must-stand-african-women-in-an-age-of-war> (accessed 10 September 2013).

81 See Anup Shah (5 January 2013) 'The arms trade is big business' Global Issues <http://www.globalissues.org/article/74/the-arms-trade-is-big-business> for details.

The 5 UN Security Council permanent members are generally the largest arms dealers ... 'Control Arms' is a campaign jointly run by Amnesty International, International Action Network on Small Arms (IANSA) and Oxfam. In a detailed report titled 'Shattered Lives' they highlight that arms are fuelling poverty and suffering, and is also out of control.

For information on arms manufacturing see <http://www.sipri.org/research/armaments/production/Top100/2011> (accessed 17 August 2013).

82 See 'Where your income tax money really goes: U.S. Federal Budget 2014 Fiscal Year' Global Day of Action on Military Spending GDAMS <http://demilitarize.org/general/income-tax-money-federal-budget-2014-fiscalyear/> accessed 12 September 2013). See also <http://www.nwtrcc.org/> (accessed 21 July 2013).

In Australia, for example, the 2012 budget wrongly allocated $190 million of defence spending as foreign aid.[83] There are other reasons for thinking the official military budget is much higher. The United States Government Accountability Office (GAO) found that in 2010 a staggering 98 Major Defense Acquisition Programs had exceeded their collective budget by $402 billion (SIPRI, n.d.).[84] That's an extra $402 billion spent on the machinery of mass death. The SIPRI also cautions on accepting the official defence budgets as the truth, and points to a systemic lack of transparency. They argue there is a lack of transparency in general information given to the public and also a lack of transparency of process. Extra and off-budget military spending occurs when other sections of the budget are colonised by defence: science or infrastructure funds, special funds for the President, loans which are paid by the Ministry of Finance, natural resource funds, corporate financial support, and more.

That almost half of the United States budget is openly and flagrantly spent on the military industrial complex—without any substantial opposition—is surely something that those who are not attached to imperialist necropolitical dogma and/or have not retreated into defeatist nihilism, should be urgently addressing.

In his famous 1961 warning about the rise of the military industrial complex, Dwight D. Eisenhower said that "every gun that is made, every warship launched, every rocket fired signifies in the final sense, a theft from those who hunger and are not fed, those who are cold and are not clothed."[85] At least

83 <http://lee-rhiannon.greensmps.org.au/content/media-releases/190m-defence-budget-blunder-carr-shouldrestore-money-afghan-aid-programs> (accessed 21 July 2013).

84 See also <http://usgovinfo.about.com/b/2006/07/27/goa-finds-security-risks-in-military-excess-equipmentsales.htm> (accessed 21 July 2013).

85 <http://coursesa.matrix.msu.edu/~hst306/documents/indust.html> (accessed 21 July 2013). See also 'War is a racket' by General Smedley Butler: "[I]t is

half of the tax that women pay in the United States is handed over to an increasingly fascist male-dominated military. While there are endless debates and protests about the government support for the banking system, and protests against cuts in welfare, health and education, the almost complete absence of debate about government funding for the military elite is bordering on sinister. Where was the debate in Australia about spending $2.94 billion on buying 12 new-build EA-18G Growler electronic attack aircraft in 2013? (Pittaway, 3 May 2013). Where was the debate when in 2010 the Australian government awarded an Order of Australia to the corporate warlord and former United States Deputy Secretary of State and CIA boss Richard Armitage?[86]

The elephant in the room is drenched with the blood of others: those distant dark-skinned others with their legs and arms blown off, who are disembowelled by bullets; mothers who cradle their children's ripped-up bodies, screaming with madness.

Every gun, warship, jet and bomb is also a theft from women as a sex class. There is more than enough money for public education, health, state-funded day-care systems, affordable housing, environmentally sustainable energy, food, and other necessities; there is more than enough money to protect single mothers and their children from deadly forms of poverty and social exclusion. *There is more than enough money.* Austerity is the propaganda of the new fascism which delivers violent budget cuts against its own citizens just as it ramps up

---

possibly the oldest, easily the most profitable, surely the most vicious. It is the only one international in scope. It is the only one in which the profits are reckoned in dollars and the losses in lives" <http://www.ratical.org/ratville/CAH/warisaracket.html> (accessed 17 August 2013).

86 For an insight into the consciousness of Armitage, his opinion of Australia and why he thinks Australia should buy American weapons of mass destruction, see Joye (19 August 2013). Here he states: "My own view is that we are the United States—we are not afraid of anything."

global inequality and steadily arms itself with weapons of mass murder.

It is possible that as a society we have not yet understood how deeply we have been conditioned into averting our minds from thinking critically or acting collectively against the massive imperial war machine that looms like a nightmare at the edges of our consciousness. If the ruling ideas of a society reflect the politics of the ruling elite, then ours are militarised values, barbarically and opportunistically sadistic. Indifference to the suffering of others is a form of sadism. Quietism, educated and tenured nihilism, hipster fatalism, defeatism, conquered and tamed passion, the socially acceptable lament that nothing works, that there are no solutions, which is often expressed with a lofty urbane sigh of disgust at the wreck of humanity, that seeps like a poison into the minds and hearts of so many— is this a form of passive collaboration with patriarchal fascism? Or are women so continually traumatised by the system that we can barely gather enough energy to think that another world might be possible? We work ourselves into the ground and, if we live in the 'land of the free', half of what we are taxed is handed to the military without our informed consent and without us knowing what the money is really used for. In one awful real sense, our exploitation is directly harvested by the military industrial complex in order to oppress, exploit, rape, murder and terrorise our sisters and their children in the east. The name given to this necropolitical exchange is 'freedom'.

There is a poem by Nâzim Hikmet, 'A Sad State of Freedom' (1951), that reminds me of the relations between women, work, freedom, capitalism and western military imperialism.

> You waste the attention of your eyes,
> the glittering labour of your hands,
> and knead dough enough for dozens of loaves,
> of which you will taste not a morsel

you are free to slave for others –
you are free to make the rich richer.
The moment you're born
they plant around you
mills that grind lies
lies to last you a lifetime.
You keep thinking in your great freedom,
a finger on your temple
free to have a free conscience.
Your head bent as if half-cut from the nape,
your arms long, hanging,
You saunter about in your great freedom:
you're free
with the freedom of being unemployed.
You love your country
as the nearest, most precious thing to you.
But one day, for example,
they may endorse it over to America,
and you, too, with your great freedom –
you have the freedom to become an air-base.
You may proclaim that one must live
not as a tool a number or a link
but as a human being –
then at once they handcuff your wrists.
You are free to be arrested, imprisoned
and even hanged.
There's neither an iron, wooden
nor a tulle curtain
in your life;
there's no need to choose freedom:
you are free.
But this kind of freedom
is a sad affair under the stars.

Exploited women in the west are free to feel empowered by a thousand glossy images of hot, kick-ass heroines with guns. Images of self-empowered femininity have become progressively militarised over the last few decades. Sexy female spies, soldiers, police officers, defence officers, trained assassins, all handling weapons as though they have finally seized (phallic) power from the 'bad boys'. These sexy combat robots are sold to us as 'feminist entertainment'. Indeed, the cover of Susan Hopkin's celebratory third wave feminist book *Girl Heroes: The New Force in Popular Culture* (2002) is a silhouette of a Barbie doll-like figure in pigtails holding a large pistol. Consider how these films eroticise and recruit support for armed conflict: *Bad Girls* (1994), *The Quick and the Dead* (1995), *La Femme Nikita* (1990), *G.I. Jane* (1997), *Tomb Raider* (2001), *Kill Bill I* (2003) and *Kill Bill II* (2004), *Mr and Mrs Smith* (2005), *Salt* (2010), and so on ad nauseam. Not to mention *Wonder Woman*, with her sexed-up star-spangled costume, *Bionic Woman* ('we have the technology'), *Charlie's Angels* and *The Avengers*. Beneath the militarised self-empowerment narrative, the dehumanising barbaric message whispered over and over again is "weapons are sexy, killing is cool." Inert, transfixed, our teeth clenched with tension, we come to enjoy the moments of death, when the baddies are killed by the goodies. We feel strangely energised emotionally as we watch them die, as though we are performing the equivalent of a salute. *Entertainment becomes war by other means.*

If the budget is dominated by the military, the imperial ideology of violence and war is everywhere celebrated in action films, horror, splatter, thrillers, violent computer games for children and teenagers, hardcore pornography, advertising which gains 'cool currency' for its authoritarian celebration of sexual violence; in the rise of snuff on the Internet, and in the steady slow-burning normalisation of fascist social values. The patriarchal capitalist entertainments industries are awash with dehumanising violence and blood.

It is perhaps the character James Bond (aka '007') who epitomises some of the exquisite thrills of militarised entertainment. In *Skyfall* (2012) James Bond fearlessly defends the interests of the imperial military elite. 'M'—eerily like Margaret Thatcher in spirit—is hunted by a revengeful former employee: a deranged, deformed, bisexual Latino terrorist hacker who, like the hacktivist collective Anonymous, operates in the shadows. The reactionary politics in the film are meant to be sexy and exciting. The film begins with a long close-up of Daniel Craig's pale blue eyes and low-hanging blond eyebrows. Salute the irrepressible fortitude, enduring superiority and sexy intelligence of the white blond master race. The film is a lavishly violent homage to numerous reactionary themes— nostalgic nationalism, the moral superiority of the Empire, xenophobia, the illegitimacy of workers' complaints, the importance of exterminating the criminal hordes (who just happen to be non-white) before they destroy the entire world, and so forth. Watch Bond running through streets bashing into people, thrusting them aside with his powerful arms, driving and crashing expensive cars, blowing up buildings and shooting and killing, in scene after scene of conspicuous destruction. Be entertained by the sophisticated wit of the British military elite as Bond remarks drily, "waste of good scotch," as a glass falls off the head of a murdered sex-slave he has recently screwed.[87] The final battle occurs in Bond's ancestral home in Scotland where the Latino invader is finally defeated when Bond throws a knife into his back. "Last rat standing," says 007 to the dying ex-employee. The film ends with a scene of fascist sentimentality, as James Bond stands triumphantly on the roof of the military intelligence headquarters in London, his profile juxtaposed with a Union Jack fluttering in the background, as though symbolically licking his face in gratitude for his heroic defence of the ruling class.

Skyfall should really be called *Chicken Little*, because throughout the film members of the elite run around frantically saying 'the sky is falling!', or rather, 'the empire is about to fall

---

87 <http://www.youtube.com/watch?v=hlBHOZkim2g> (accessed 23 August 2013).

at the hands of a campy Latino anarchist hacker!' Nasty politics and violence sexed-up with a misogynistic military killer are meant to be Xtremely entertaining. This is the kind of film during which one eats a supersize serving of salty popcorn—washed down with a supersize serving of Coke.

Images of skulls, which were once the insignia of Nazi death squads, are now cool and worn with pride on clothes and jewellery made in sweatshops in poor Asian countries by women and children whose governments have lowered their heads before the big-guns of so-called western democracies.

Mesmerised, traumatised or merely stunned by the spectacle of a violence that is so relentless, we come to think of it as inevitable; we barely notice that there is no real transparency or debate about defence spending thinking, perhaps, that these billions are about protecting us. But the bloated defence budget is not about keeping us safe; it is, first of all, an act of blatant socio-economic warfare against those of us living in the west, and secondly, an act of overt imperial violence against the rest of humanity.

In 2010 the International Peace Bureau (IPB) founded the Global Day of Action on Military Spending.[88] In 2013, 155 actions occurred in 124 cities in 24 countries. The Facebook Inc. website indicates, through photographs of these actions, that they were small-scale. The Women's International League for Peace and Freedom (WILPF) supported the Global Day of Action on Military Spending (15 April 2013) as part of their 'Challenging Militarism' program. Their website states:

> In 2011 global military spending surged to US 1.74 trillion. In Australia military spending is currently $25 billion a year and rising. Given the crisis facing the planet—economic, environmental, health, food—we must create a global movement to shift this money to human needs. There are millions who support this point of view.

---

88 See <http://demilitarize.org/about/> (accessed 21 July 2013).

Over 80% of Australians don't want more of their taxes spent on the military.[89]

And as Judith Le Blanc from the US Peace Action states: "*We need a movement that is global and grassroots, that will take action, educate and generate an alternative vision for global economic security for all*" (emphasis in original).[90]

If the true cost of the defence budget to human life and the environment were carefully elaborated and exposed and became something that was continually and rigorously discussed, then the beginning of an important change in consciousness would happen. Opposition to the Poll Tax in the United Kingdom in the 1980s was vigorous, and it is possible that opposition to the defence budget could create an even stronger movement. In effect, the defence budget is a tax, which is far more destructive to communities than the Poll Tax or the Goods and Services Tax (GST). A mass movement of conscientious objection to paying tax money to the military industrial complex would achieve, at the very least, an awareness of what is going on. No tax for war. No money for murder. Not in our name.

Protesting against the thuggery and gangsterism of imperial wars cooked up by generals, global banks and corporations has limited impact when their lifeblood, the national defence budget, remains in place. *We are their lifeblood*, they depend on our ignorance, exploitation, terror, complicity and tax dollars for their money. As Felix Guattari writes in 'To have done with the massacre of the body':

[W]e can no longer permit our nervous systems to serve as a communications network for the system of capitalist exploitation,

89 <http://www.wilpf.org.au/> and <http://demilitarize.org/wp-content/uploads/2013/06/gdams-2013-full-reportfinal. pdf> (accessed 21 July 2013).

90 <http://demilitarize.org/wp_content/uploads/2013/06/gdams-2013-full-report-final.pdf> (accessed 21 July 2013). Global Day of Action on Military Spending announced that "[t]he cross-cutting message was: Cut the military budget and fund human needs."

for the patriarchal state; nor can we permit our brains to be used as instruments of torture programmed by the powers that surround us (2009b, p. 209).

Transparency about weapons and how they kill people is also needed. What exactly are these multi-billion dollar EA-18G Growler electronic attack aircraft, and how do they kill people? Why must they be bought? What are the imperial politics behind the Talisman Saber training exercise which occurs twice a year and brings together 28,000 United States and Australian military personnel? Do we naively trust the generals when they tell us that it is all for our own good, and not to worry our little sheeple[91] civilian heads about things we do not understand when the money they take from us is forcing us into dangerous levels of poverty? They march around in circles, looking extremely serious wearing ridiculous uniforms and hats, covered in badges of eagles, crowns, stars, rifles, swords and wings. They give each other medals in very important ceremonies full of flags. They stand to attention and salute, click their heels and spin around with straight backs. They do this hundreds of times. They carry guns and have big, shiny boots. They give each other names, such as Admiral, Marshal, General, Commodore, Brigadier, and Lieutenant Colonel. They continually lie to the public, fund and train dictatorships. It's all very Top Secret and Classified Information while the private information of civilians is spied on by the National Security Agency and PRISM.[92]

Haven't they got enough weapons from last year? Why on earth do they need all this money every year? Why do the governments give obscene amount of money to defence

91 "1. Sheeple: People unable to think for themselves. Followers. Lemmings. Those with no cognitive abilities of their own" <www.urbandictionary.com/define.php?term=sheeple> (accessed 17 August 2013).

92 For information on PRISM, the Internet data-mining system connected to the NSA which Edward Snowden disclosed, see Kelley (8 July 2013).

instead of paying off their debts? Is someone holding a gun to *their* heads? A 2013 report from the Transnational Institute (TNI) argues that while the German government has forced social cuts to other EU members it

> ... has been lobbying behind the scenes against cuts to military spending in countries such as Greece because of concerns for its own arms industry and the debt it's owed ... An aide to former Greek Prime Minister George Papandreou, has reportedly said: 'No-one is saying "Buy our warships or we won't bail you out." But the clear implication is that they will be more supportive if we do' ... European leaders such as David Cameron and Francois Hollande have become travelling salespeople for their arms industries, promoting to countries with questionable human rights records (Hall, 2013, p. 22).[93]

Exactly what kind of influence do the military industrial complex and the vastly powerful global arms corporations have over the governments and the mass media? Who will stop them if we don't?

The women's liberation movement was once actively involved in combating the patriarchal capitalist war machine, for example, in the anti-Vietnam and anti-nuclear movements of the 1970s and 1980s. "Challenging militarism is essential for a feminist revolution," write the anonymous authors of 'Feminist Revolutionary Force for Change' (1985, p. 17). The co-founder of the American National Organisation of Women (NOW), Sheila Tobias (1985), identified the defence budget as a key feminist issue in the 1980s. Sadly, her important arguments have since been marginalised. However, the International Peace Bureau now has a platform called 'Disarmament for development—sustainable disarmament for

---

93 See also: Slijper (2013) 'Guns, debt and corruption'; Anup Shah (2013) Global Issues <http://www.globalissues.org/article/74/the-arms-trade-is-big-business> (accessed 12 September 2013); Rettman (2012) 'EU figures show crisis-busting arms sales to Greece'; Smith (2012) 'German "hypocrisy" over Greek military spending'.

sustainable development'.[94] In short, take the money from the military and give it back to the people. Radically questioning and blocking the defence budget could function as a much stronger point of solidarity for many political tribes in the anti-globalisation movement. Currently, there is much endless debate among feminist groups about how to create solidarity, how to negotiate differences and reach consensus. These conversations are made in the shadow of an imperial military elite that is rarely acknowledged. The continuum of male violence reaches its most horrific and powerful expression in the military industrial complex, and it brings with it massive environmental destruction and economic imperialism.[95] Few realise that "[t]he military are the world's largest source of carbon emissions, so posing one of the most ignored threats to planetary sustainability" (Mama, 2012, p. 29–30).

Amina Mama is one of the leading voices in a new group of international feminist scholars and activists who are exposing the global degradation brought about by militarism and drawing urgent attention to the need for a broader feminist engagement with the problem of industrialised male violence (see for example Young, 2003; Lutz, 2002, 2009; Enloe, 2000, 2007; Cock, 1992; Cockburn, 2007, Barry, 2010, Hawthorne and Winter, 2002). As Amina Mama writes:

> Militarism constitutes a formidable obstacle to equity, development and freedom, both within the militarist-exporting nations (like the USA) and the beneficiaries of these exports where the violent conflicts take place. Militarised developing countries accumulate severe debts, only to draw further on foreign military assistance that is readily available and which sustains this deadly global industry, while the true costs are paid in loss of lives, basic freedoms and the long-term deformation of human potential ... At the global level, military costs

---

94 See <http://www.ipb.org/web> (accessed 21 July 2013).

95 On the huge, yet rarely discussed, carbon footprint of the military industrial complex, see <http://www.greenbiz.com/news/2010/04/23/us-military-battles-massive-carbon-footprint> (accessed 18 August 2013).

are exempt from the regulation of international trade organisations like the WTO. Yet both the investments and the costs are huge and the outcomes affect everybody, not just the military. More people-centred approaches to governance are likely to be more attentive to the human costs of increasing global inequities (between rich and poor nations) and thus to the threat that this entrenched spending pattern poses to democratic and people-centred development, as well as to the developmental inequities that are part and parcel of the global norms of excessive and competitive investment in the military (Mama, 2012, p. 42).

Importantly, a radical opposition to the defence budget could bring together 'first' and 'third world' women. Maria Mies has argued that

> ... the feminist struggles against male violence, against rape, wife-beatings, the molestation and humiliation of women, have been rallying points for women in First and Third World countries. The literature on these issues has been translated and read in many countries. Women can identify with 'the other woman' across class, racial and imperialist barriers, if they have begun themselves to struggle against male violence (1986/1998, p. 230).

But we also need to challenge the larger expression of male violence, the imperialist barrier between poor and rich nations which is best illustrated in the west's military industrial complex that bombs the homes of women, rapes, kills, pollutes, threatens, coerces. It is, surely, the responsibility of women in the west to challenge the militarised patriarchy of the rich that oppresses women in the poor nations. Mama draws attention in her work to women's anti-war activism in places such as Nigeria, Ghana, Liberia and Sierra Leone, to women who risk their lives overcoming armed conflict which is all too frequently funded and supported by the west and which results in the mass rape and death of children and women. As Nighat Said Khan from Pakistan writes:

The onus of a global movement, including a global women's movement, lies with the North since even the combined struggle of the South will not, and cannot, be successful in bringing about global change in what is called the new world order, since this ordering is determined by a handful of countries and significantly by the United States. We in the South can do our best but until the women's movement and feminist academics in the North are also against their respective states and the international world order, we will never see a global women's movement (Khan, 2004, p. 86).

Why not aim for consensus on disarming the defence budget? Why not calculate the costs to the women and children of the world, and the environment in general, of letting the parasitic blood-bloated tick of the military industrial complex feed off our bodies forever?

5.1 Resisting Necropolitics

To thoroughly resist the indignity of necropolitics would require a sustained, organised, indignant cultural revolution that expelled the fascist within from his seat of control by naming and resisting the social chemistry of necropolitics. It would mean decoding a hegemonic necropolitics that saturates all social relations, from the tyrannical dynamics of familialism, sex, banking, money, consumption, workplace hierarchies, the entertainment industry, academia, media, to the prison system, medical, educational and juridical apparatus, through to the overt ideological machinery of war. It would require developing a nose for the stench of dead flesh that wafts from government documents, workplace contracts, the TV, the Internet, shops; and an eye for the deadly exploitation of others hidden behind a thousand advertisements for the system that recruit our minds from every direction.

Catherine Lutz identifies militarism as

... the contradictory and tense social process in which civil society organizes itself for the production of violence ... This process involves an intensification of the labor and resources allocated to military purposes, including the shaping of other institutions in synchrony with military goals. Militarization is simultaneously a discursive process, involving a shift in general societal beliefs and values in ways necessary to legitimate the use of force, the organization of large standing armies and their leaders, and the higher taxes or tribute used to pay for them (2002, p. 5).

In what ways have our western institutions become synchronised with military goals? How are our emotions recruited by necropolitics?

The ideology of militarisation has many expressions—the blood and soil rhetoric of nationalism is the most obvious, routinely celebrated in sporting events where jingoism is disguised as healthy athletic competition. The marketing of mass violence as entertainment is another obvious glorification of the senseless barbarism that drives militarisation. Less obvious examples are the third wave neo–liberal kick–ass fictional feminist heroines with guns (Lara Croft is one of them) and their real-life versions of female politicians and corporate power brokers who support the financing of armed conflict. Even less obvious, perhaps, is the militarisation of ecological discourses that buy into the neo–eugenicist narratives about an impending population explosion.

A paradigmatic example of this trend was visible on the front cover of the 30 June 2013 issue of *The New Review*, the weekend magazine for *The Observer*, a UK paper with a high-brow left-wing aura. The cover carried a large photograph of a solemn white man holding the globe in his hand in a gesture that quotes hundreds of depressed Hamlets talking to skulls. However, instead of a skull, there is the earth in his hand. But the accompanying edited extract[96] from Stephen Emmott's book *Ten Billion* (2013) is less Shakespearian than a vulgar neo–eugenicist rant that wears the respectable fig leaf of

---

96 Emmott (30 June 2013)

environmentalism. The published (hard copy) extract carries a photograph of Emmott standing to attention, his arms stiffly by his sides, dwarfed and outnumbered by photographs of giant non-white babies in nappies, the largest of whom has dark brown-coloured skin and looms over the text. Concerns about climate change, he argues, are always concerns about the threat posed to the earth by an expanding population. A list of predominantly non-white countries terrifies a predominantly white readership with alarming figures about massive population explosions. As a favourable review in *The Guardian* puts it: "[E]very aspect of the environmental crisis is interconnected and all flow from the pressure of population" (Gray, 5 July 2013).

In the extract from his book Emmott argues that soon a huge tide of "climate migrants" will flood the world. First world countries, he speculates, "may well look like something approaching militarised countries, with heavily defended border controls" (2013, p. 10). The extract in *The Observer* ends on an ominous note:

We might rightly call the situation we're in an unprecedented emergency. We urgently need to do—and I mean actually do—something radical to avert a global catastrophe. But I don't think we will, I think we're fucked. I asked one of the most rational, brightest scientists I know—a scientist working in this area, a young scientist, a scientist in my lab—if there was just one thing he had to do about the situation we face, what would it be? His reply? 'Teach my son how to use a gun' (Emmott, 30 June 2013, p. 11).

Having tried to convince the reader that this is an apolitical opinion by repeating the word 'scientist' four times, Emmott's by proxy solution to what he thinks will be the invasion of 'climate immigrants', otherwise known as 'immigrants' or 'refugees', is teaching young men in western countries how to shoot. In short, shooting immigrants is advocated in the name of ecological concern. And the review in *The Guardian* supports this neo-fascist alarmism:

> Emmott tells us that the violent spillover of environmental crisis is attracting the concern of military thinkers, and reports a young scientific colleague telling him that, looking ahead, he plans to teach his son how to use a gun. A course in computer hacking might be more useful, but the point is sound (Gray, 5 July 2013).

Here human beings are not even called 'climate immigrants' or 'immigrants', they become instead 'the violent spillover', as though they themselves are the source of violence. One must arm oneself against the impending hordes of brown-skinned immigrants who will soon destroy not only the earth itself, but also civilisation as we—in the rich westernised countries—know it. And of course, it is the mothers in poor countries who are the source of this 'violent spillover'. The idea that the population of poor nations needs to be forcibly controlled has, historically, resulted in the violent oppression of women's bodies. As Renate Klein and colleagues put it:

> [A] feminist critique of the logic of domination that underlies population control policies clearly rejects any form of population control—feminist or otherwise. Instead of using the rhetoric of 'choice' and 'reproductive rights' we demand an examination of the ideology 'bullets turned into contraceptives' (1991/2013, p. lxxxvii).

Racism and misogyny are expressions of necropolitics. And racist inflected misogyny is building, just as fascist social values become normalised.

Consider some of the comments made about Marion Bartoli (French professional tennis player) during and after Wimbledon 2013. Bartoli does not conform to the thin, tall, blond tennis star look and for this she was subjected to abuse. She was called an "oily French faced bitch," a "fat ugly smelly little slut," "fat greasy bitch," a "fucking dyke," a "fat lesbian looking lump of shit," a "disrespectful masculine whore."[97] Some men threatened to rape and kill her and expressed a strong desire that she would die.

These comments are political statements, declarations of war against women who do not conform to an Aryan ideal. They are a crude mainstream version of the politics expressed in a neo-Nazi website Great White Desert:

> This new Aryan woman, however, is most certainly not the strident, sometimes lesbian, often race-mixing Marxist-loving woman, or career-minded, selfishly aggressive woman that modern 'feminism' desires to create, for such 'feminist' women have no notion of racial duty, no honour, no love of Aryan culture and certainly no genuine Aryan spirit … It is no coincidence that those at the forefront of the campaign for so-called 'feminism' are Marxists and Jews. Indeed, the whole women's liberation movement' was the creation of Jews.[98]

If Bartoli's body had conformed to the Aryan ideal of femininity she would not have been abused in the way she was. Here, as with the white supremacist conspiracy theory about feminism, homophobic misogyny expresses itself as a form of neo-Nazi hatred of the non-blond female. Misogyny and fascism have always been closely connected.

---

97 <http://publicshaming.tumblr.com/post/54864863081/womens-wimbledon-champion-marion-bartoli-deemed> (accessed 21 July 2013). See also Melinda Tankard Reist, *The Age* (13 July 2013) 'The ugly truth is rules are different for girls in sport' <http://www.theage.com.au/comment/the-ugly-truth-is-rules-are-different-for-girls-in-sport-20130713-2pwhc.html> and also <http://www.independent.co.uk/news/media/tv-radio/john-inverdale-sends-personal-apology-to-marion-bartoli-over-never-going-to-be-a-looker-remark-8693585.html> (accessed 17 August 2013).

98 <http://greatwhitedesert.org/dir/index.php?title=The_Duty_of_Aryan_Women> (accessed 17 August 2013).

5.2 To Resist Here so They Can Live Better There

In her important classic *Patriarchy and Accumulation on a World Scale: Women and the International Division of Labour* (1986/1998) Maria Mies proposes that a feminist consumer liberation movement practise the ethos of *"ici vivre mieux/la-bas vaincre la faim* [To live better here and to fight hunger there]" (p. 228). She writes that

> ... this slogan expresses the desire that the definition of what the 'good life' or human happiness is should no longer be left to the lieutenants of transnational capital, but that we ourselves begin to define it (p. 228).

I talk to a friend in Copenhagen, who often hangs out in an inner-city collective 'Freetown Christiania' (a commune of 34 hectares and almost 900 people which began in 1971 when people took over an abandoned military base) and we imagine an alternative culture where everything is shared and no one owns anything. We dream of new living practices and non-nuclear-family social relations, of public housing full of people who share resources, money, clothes, labour, where children are brought up by many adults not just their biological parents, where it does not matter who the biological father is, and the idea of a 'single mother' makes no sense. It's a life in which there is no sense of sexual ownership, or bourgeois monogamy, and no sexual division of labour in the home. We imagine apartment buildings of vibrant sharing communities, no locks, no thieves, shared food, washing machines. Where the creepy privacy of the male-dominated nuclear family no longer festers with secret crimes, and where there is no more domestic violence because everyone would know about it straight away and everyone would stop it.

We imagine gardens and fields that are farmed collectively, where wild seeds flourish and bees are not full of chemicals. We imagine collective cars and buses, the use of many bikes.

We imagine communities that practise the collective care of the young, sick, weak and old. Communities where women are honoured for being able to give birth to life, and are no longer objectified, beaten or abused. Wild and joyful women-only communities. And communities where there are no more paranoid psychic and physical fences between ages, ethnicities, sexes, races and abilities. Where people are listened to and hugged when they are sad, without having to pay a stranger to listen to them or take poisonous pills for their brains. A thousand different off-grid communities, each one unique and fluid. A vast horizontal collective that is held together by the basic humane principles of dignity, compassion, respect, sharing, and non-violence. We imagine common land farmed in sustainable ways, bartering systems, a multitude of alternative autonomous communities that practise ethical consumption, a mass consumer boycotting. The creation of a 'good life' that is also an active protest against neo-liberal globalisation.[99]

We also imagine feminist flash-mobbing of corporate kings, IMF and World Bank executives, of men in high places. We imagine creating an international mourning month for all women and children who are raped and killed by men, the wearing of black bands, solemn marches, a month of silence, a general refusal to engage in sadosociety, a deep historical grieving. We imagine the creation of a movement which takes over abandoned houses and empty buildings for use by the homeless; mass hunger strikes, suffragette-style civil disobedience; industrial action led by women in the secondary labour market and the unemployed; the picketing of welfare departments and buildings; the mass circulation of off-grid power solutions; generators made from recycled cars, computers, washing machines; food co-operatives run from homes; specialist such as doctors, teachers, lawyers, artisans,

---

99 For further inspiration about the 'good life' see Maria Mies (2010) *The Village and the World.*

who exchange their labour with others; the growth of non-money economies.

But none of these practices dislodge the military tick that feeds off the women in rich western countries in order to oppress and kill the women of other nations. Retreating into an oasis of ethical living and consumption within a heavily militarised imperialist patriarchal culture might save the sanity and health of people here, but will have little impact on the lives of women and children elsewhere.

Consumer boycotting, shaming advertisers into withdrawing sponsorship, media activism, grassroots campaigning, are all vital actions, but again, much of this violent misogyny is supported, even outright funded, by the intensely creepy global military network which is protected by transnational banks, governments, and global corporations. What is needed is a "genuine security" for all, an end to all forms of violence including rape and domestic violence during so-called peacetime.[100]

Misogyny has been re-loaded by those who profit from death and the living death of extreme exploitation—the intensifying barbarism of misogyny is the cultural logic of the new global fascism. The rise of the new fascism and the war against women brings new energy to the old rebel call DEMAND THE IMPOSSIBLE. What is required is a fearless *loving* solidarity against every form of necropolitics, from the micropolitics of social violence, exclusion, exploitation, symbolic and actual violence against women to the macropolitics

---

100 As Amina Mama writes:

> The International Network of Women Against Militarism advocates 'genuine security', a concept that, like human security includes economic, educational and other human development concerns, but which specifically addresses security from women's perspectives. These include gender equity which includes freedom from rape and domestic violence in peacetime as much as in wartime, on the basis that women need to feel secure in their homes and on the streets, as well as bringing about an end to war (2012, p. 43).

of industrialised mass murder. As Amina Mama puts it so clearly and powerfully: "The greatest threat to women (and by extension humanity) is the growth and acceptance of a misogynistic, authoritarian and violent culture of militarism."[101] Another world *is* possible if, to paraphrase Martin Luther King, women who want an end to the global affliction of militarised male violence learn to organise as effectively as those who control the spread of militarism.[102]

Some might say that seeking to disarm the empire of patriarchal capitalism is both reformist and naïve. Reformist, because it merely modifies an inherently barbaric system which is founded on the grotesque exploitation of human life, and life in general; or even that an authentic revolution requires a people's army, weapons to 'defend' rights with, to kill with (forgetting perhaps the impact of the arms race on the destruction of an alternative to capitalism). Naïve, because it is as idealistic and silly as the beautiful teen gesture of gracefully silencing the mouth of a gun with a red carnation; and after all, let's get real, as the tamed and obedient pessimists so often say, 'they have won' and another world will never be possible; the best we can hope for is less violence, especially in our backyard.

But we have blood on our hands, *The Blood of Others*, to cite the title of Simone de Beauvoir's (1945) anti-war novel about the French resistance: we are inhabited by a fascism we have yet to name. Until we begin the painful collective work of resisting our own fascism, our as yet unexplored complicity with our Empire of Barbarism—even as feminists—the dream

---

101 <http://www.africanfeministforum.com/quotes-from-voice-power-and-soul/> (accessed 20 August 2013).

102 Martin Luther King, in his 25 February 1967 speech at The Nation Institute, Los Angeles, 'The casualties of the war in Vietnam' said: "Those of us who love peace must learn to organise as effectively as the war hawks. As they spread the propaganda of war we must spread the propaganda of peace" <http://www.aavw.org/specialfeatures/speeches_king02.html> (accessed 10 September 2013).

of peace, of an end to male domination through violence, will be continually sabotaged by our own too often disavowed desire to fight each other. Disarming those who protect the system, raising awareness of how a shadowy military industrial complex not only defends the interests of the ruling elite, but governs it, is rapidly emerging as an urgent priority.

Wake up sister; fascism has you.

Acknowledgements

Thank you to the following people for wisdom, friendship, inspiration, dialogue, laughter, food, and love. Korosh Azizi, Mischa Bray, Jodi Chettoe, Hugh Chettoe, Dane Craig, Didier Filia, Anth Ginn, Dot Ginn, Charity Haynes, Susan Hawthorne, Renate Klein, Ann-Claire Larsen, Robyn Mandal, James R. Marsh, Jeffrey Masson, David M, Yvette Rocheron, Caroline S. Taylor, Melinda Tankard Reist, Vivien Encel and Vagelis Z.

To my poor and unemployed friends who somehow, with great dignity, manage a precarious existence on the margins—in honour of their political wisdom and passion for justice, for their friendship and elegant generosity.

To the women at Spinifex: Danielle for editorial input; Pauline for excellent mistake spotting, Maree for brilliant copy editing. Deb for the audacious cover. And many thanks especially to Susan and Renate for their patience and faith.

Bibliography

Adorno, Theodor W. and Max Horkheimer (1992) *Dialectic of Enlightenment*, trans. John Cumming. Verson, London and New York.

Agamben, Giorgio (1998) *Homo Sacre: Sovereign Power and Bare Life*, trans. Danile Heller-Roazen. Stanford University Press, Stanford.

Agel, Jerome (1971) *The Radical Therapist: The Therapist Collective*. Ballantine Books, New York.

Arendt, Hannah (1994) *Essays in Understanding, 1930–1954*, ed. Jerome Kohn. Harcourt & Brace, New York.

Argov, Sherry (2006) *Why Men Marry Bitches: A Woman's Guide to Winning Her Man's Heart*. Simon & Schuster, London.

Arnot, Margaret L. (1994) 'Infant death, child care and the state: The baby-farming scandal and the first infant life protection legislation of 1872' *Continuity and Change* 9 (2), pp. 271–311.

Bad Girls (1994) motion picture, 20th Century Fox, USA. Director Jonathan Kaplan; producer Charles Finch.

Barry, Kathleen (2010) *Unmaking War. Remaking Men*. Phoenix Rising Press, Santa Rosa; Spinifex Press, North Melbourne.

Bartlett, Alison (2013) 'Feminist protest and cultural production at the Pine Gap women's protest camp, 1983' *Women: A Cultural Review* 24 (2-3), pp. 179–195.

Beauboeuf-Lafontant, Tamara (2007) 'You have to show strength: An exploration of gender, race and depression' *Gender & Society* 21 (1), pp. 28–51.

Beckwith, J.B. (1993) 'Gender stereotypes and mental health revisited' *Social Behavior and Personality* 21 (1), pp. 85–88.

Belknap, Joanne (2010) 'Rape: Too hard to report and too easy to discredit victims' *Violence Against Women* 16 (12), pp. 1,335–1,344.

Binding, Karl and Alfred Hoche (2012) [First published 1920] *Die Freigabe der Vernichtung lebensunwerten Lebens* [Allowing the Destruction of Life Unworthy of Life], trans. Cristina Modak. Suzeteo Enterprises, USA.

Bindley, Katherine (16 November 2011) 'Women and prescription drugs' *Huffington Post* <http://www.huffingtonpost.com/2011/11/16/women-and-prescription-drug-use_n_1098023.html> (accessed 21st July 2013).

Booth, Heather (13 November 2006) 'Remarks', Meeting of the Veteran Feminists of America, Columbia University Faculty House, New York City.

Bradshaw, John (1992) *Homecoming: Reclaiming Your Inner Child.* Bantam Books, London.

Bray, Abigail (24 August 2009) 'Googling s*x' *On Line Opinion* <http://www.onlineopinion.com.au/view.asp?article=9344> (accessed 21 July 2013).

Bray, Abigail (2011) 'The pornification of post-feminism: Why Roddick's $ex shops are a sell out' in Melinda Tankard Reist and Abigail Bray (eds) *Big Porn Inc: Exposing the Harms of the Global Pornography Industry.* Spinifex Press, North Melbourne, pp. 118–121.

Breggin, Peter R. (1998) 'Electroshock: Scientific, ethical, and political issues' *International Journal of Risk & Safety in Medicine* 11, pp. 5–40.

Breggin, Peter R. (31 October 2009) 'Antipsychotic drugs, their harmful effects, and the limits of tort reform' *The Huffington Post* <http://www.huffingtonpost.com/dr-peter-breggin/antipsychotic-drugs-their_b_341108.html> (accessed 21 July 2013).

Breggin, Peter R. (2011) 'Psychiatric drug-induced Chronic Brain Impairment (CBI): Implications for long-term treatment with psychiatric medication' *International Journal of Risk & Safety in Medicine* 23, pp. 193–200.

Brenner, Johanna (2000) *Women and the Politics of Class.* Monthly Review Press, New York.

Brinkley, John R., Bernard D. Beitmen, Robert O. Friedel (1979) 'Low-dose neuroleptic regimens in the treatment of borderline patients' *Archives of General Psychiatry* 36 (3), pp. 319–326.

Broverman, Inge K., Donald M. Broverman, Frank E. Clarkson, Paul S. Rosenkrantz, and Susan R. Vogel (1970) 'Sex role stereotypes and clinical judgements of mental health' *Journal of Consulting and Clinical Psychology* 34 (1), pp.1–7.

Brownmiller, Susan (1975) *Against Our Will: Men, Women and Rape.* Penguin Books, Harmondsworth.

Burke, Jason, Amelia Gentleman and Philip Willan (1 October 2000) 'British link to "snuff" videos' *The Guardian/The Observer* <http://www.theguardian.com/uk/2000/oct/01/ameliagentleman.philipwillan> (accessed 6 August 2013).

Burns, Melinda (28 October 2010) 'Welfare reforms failing poor single mothers' *Pacific Standard* <http://www.psmag.com/politics/welfare-reform-failing-poor-single-mothers-24778/> (accessed 17 August 2013).

Byrne, Rhonda (2006) *The Secret.* Atria Books/Beyond Words, New York.

Castleman, Michael (16 March 2009) 'The most important sexual statistic' *Psychology Today* <http://www.psychologytoday.com/blog/all-about-sex/200903/the-most-important-sexual-statistic> (accessed 21 July 2013).

Chan, Wendy, Dorothy E. Chunn, Robert Menzies (eds) (2012) *Women, Madness and the Law: A Feminist Reader*. Routledge, New York and London.

Chesler, Phyllis (1972) *Women and Madness*. Penguin Books, Harmondsworth.

Chopper (2000) motion picture, Australian Film Finance Corporation, Sydney. Director Andrew Dominic.

Church, Mark (5 January 2013) 'Australian Government cuts welfare payments to single parents' World Socialist Web Site <http://www.wsws.org/en/articles/2013/01/05/pove-j05.html> (accessed 16 August 2013).

Citizens Commission on Human Rights International (n.d.) Chemical Labotomy <http://www.cchrint.org/tag/chemical-lobotomy/> (accessed 21 July 2013).

Clinton, Bill (22 August 2006) 'How we ended welfare, together' *The New York Times* <http://www.nytimes.com/2006/08/22/opinion/22clinton.html?_r=0 (accessed 14 August 2013).

Cock, Jacklyn (1992) *Women and War in South Africa*. Open Letters, London.

Cockburn, Cynthia (2007) *From Where We Stand: Women's Activism and Feminist Analysis*. Zed Books, London and New York.

Collins, Jane J. and Victoria Mayer (2010) *Both Hands Tied: Welfare Reform and the Race to the Bottom in the Low-Wage Labor Market*. Chicago University Press, Chicago.

de Beauvoir, Simone (1945/1964) *The Blood of Others*. Penguin in association with Martin Secker & Warburg Ltd, London.

Deep Throat (1972) motion picture, Bryanston Pictures, USA. Director Jerry Gerard; producer Lou Perry.

Denning, Michael (2010) 'Wageless life' *New Left Review* <http://newleftreview.org/II/66/michael-denning-wageless-life> (accessed 21 July 2013).

Desclos, Anne (1954/2013) *The Story of O*. Random House, London.

Douglas, Susan R. (2010) *Enlightened Sexism: The Seductive Message that Feminism's Work Is Done*. Time Books, London.

Durrant, Sabine (11 June 2008) 'Are men boring?' *Intelligent Life* <http://moreintelligentlife.com/story/are-men-boring> (accessed 21 July 2013).

Ehrenreich, Barbara (2009) *Smile or Die: How Positive Thinking Fooled America and the World*. Granta, London.

Ehrenreich, Barbara and Deirdre English (1989) *For Her Own Good: 150 Years of the Experts' Advice to Women*. Doubleday, New York and London.

Eisenstein, Hester (2009) *Feminism Seduced: How Global Elites Use Women's Labor and Ideas to Exploit the World*. Paradigm Publishers, London and Boulder.

Ellis, Brett Easton (1991) *American Psycho*. Vintage Books, New York.

Emmott, Stephen (2013) *Ten Billion*. Penguin Books, London.

Emmott, Stephen (30 June 2013) 'Humans: The real threat to life on Earth' *The Observer*. Also at: <http://www.theguardian.com/environment/2013/jun/30/stephen-emmott-ten-billion> (accessed 7 September 2013).

Enloe, Cynthia (2000) *Maneuvers: The International Politics of Militarizing Women's Lives*. University of California Press, Berkeley and Los Angeles.

Enloe, Cynthia (2007) *Globalization and Militarism: Feminists Make the Link*. Rowman & Littlefield Publishers, New York.

Fanon, Frantz (1968) *The Wretched of the Earth*, trans. C. Farrington. Penguin Books, New York; MacGibbon & Kee, Aylesbury.

Fatal Attraction (1987) motion picture, Paramount Pictures, California. Director Adrian Lyne; producers Stanley J. Jaffe, Sherry Lansing.

Fayard, Nicole and Yvette Rocheron (2011) '"Moi quand on dit qu'une femme ment, eh bien, elle ment". The administration of rape in twenty-first century France and England & Wales' *French Politics, Culture and Society* 29 (1), pp. 68–92.

Fein, Ellen and Sherrie Schneider (1995) *The Rules: Time-tested Secrets for Capturing the Heart of Mr Right*. Grand Central Publisher, Warner Books, New York.

'Feminist Revolutionary Force for Change' (1985) in *We Are Ordinary Women: A Chronicle of the Puget Sound Women's Peace Camp* by Participants of the Puget Sound Women's Peace Camp. Seal Press, Seattle.

Fincher, Leta Hong (11 October 2012) 'China's leftover women' *New York Times* <http://www.nytimes.com/2012/10/12/opinion/global/chinas-leftover-women.html?_r=0> (accessed 21 July 2013).

Fisher, Bonnie S., Francis T. Cullen and Michael G. Turner (2000) 'The sexual victimization of college women', Research Report, National Institute of Justice, Bureau of Justice Statistics, Department of Justice, Washington, DC.

Fisher, Bonnie S., Leah E. Daigle, Francis T. Cullen, and Michael G. Turner (2003) 'Reporting sexual victimization to the police and others: Results from a national-level study of college women' *Criminal Justice and Behavior* 30 (1), pp. 6–38.

Frank, Thomas (1997) *The Conquest of Cool: Business, Culture, Counterculture, and the Rise of Hip Consumerism*. University of Chicago Press, Chicago.

Frank, Thomas (2001) *One Market Under God: Extreme Capitalism, Market Populism and the End of Economic Democracy*. Secker & Warburg, London.

Freire, Paulo (1977) *Pedagogy of the Oppressed*, trans. Myra Bergman Ramos. Penguin Books, Harmondsworth.

Friedan, Betty (1963/1983) *The Feminine Mystique*. Dell Publishing, New York.

Friedel, Robert O. (2004) *Borderline Personality Disorder Demystified*. Marlowe & Camps, New York.

G.I. Jane (1997) motion picture, Hollywood Pictures, USA. Director and producer Ridley Scott.

Gill, Rosalind (2008) 'Culture and subjectivity in neoliberal and postfeminist times' *Subjectivity* 25, pp. 425–445.

Gill, Rosalind and Elena Herdieckerhoff (2006) 'Rewriting the romance: New femininities in chick lit?' <http://eprints.lse.ac.uk/2514/1/ Rewritingtherom.pdf>, pp. 1–28.

Gloor, Peter (2010) *Coolfarming: Turn Your Great Idea into the Next Big Thing*. AMACOM Books, New York.

Gold, Tanya (19 August 2011) 'Single mothers UK riots' *The Guardian* <http://www.guardian.co.uk/commentisfree/2011/aug/19/single-mothers-uk-riots-tanya-gold> (accessed 21 July 2013).

Gordon, Linda (1994) *Pitied But Not Entitled: Single Mothers and the History of Welfare, 1890–1935*. Harvard University Press, Cambridge MA.

Gray, John (5 July 2013) '*Ten Billion* by Stephen Emmott – Review' *The Guardian* <http://www.guardian.co.uk/books/2013/jul/05/ten-billion-stephen-emmott-review> (accessed 21 July 2013).

Greer, Germaine (1970) *The Female Eunuch*. MacGibbon & Kee Ltd, Aylesbury.

Greer, Germaine (1999) *The Whole Woman*. Transworld Publishers, London.

Greer, Germaine (2012) 'Do you feel any more confident yet?' Stuff.co.nz <http://www.stuff.co.nz/life-style/beauty/8089012/Do-you-feel-any-more-confident-yet> (accessed 21 July 2013).

Guattari, Felix (2009a) 'Everybody wants to be a fascist' in *Chaosophy: Texts and Interviews 1972–1977*, ed. Sylvere Lotringer; intro. Francois Dosse; trans. David L. Sweet, Jarres Becker, Taylor Adkins. Semiotext(e), Los Angeles, pp. 154–175.

Guattari, Felix (2009b) 'To have done with the massacre of the body' in *Chaosophy: Texts and Interviews 1972–1977*, ed. Sylvere Lotringer; intro. Francois Dosse; trans. David L. Sweet, Jarres Becker, Taylor Adkins. Semiotext(e), Los Angeles, pp. 207–214.

Hall, Amy (July/August 2013) 'Austerity hypocrisy: Military spending is spared the chop' *New Internationalist*, p. 22.

Hallett, Stephanie (2 May 2011) '25 facts about rape in America' *Ms. Magazine* <http://msmagazine.com/blog/2011/05/02/25-facts-about-rape-in-america/> (accessed 15 August 2013).

Harvey, David (2005) *A Brief History of Neoliberalism*. Oxford University Press, Oxford.

Hawthorne, Susan (2002) *Wild Politics: Feminism, Globalisation and Bio/diversity*. Spinifex Press, North Melbourne.

Hawthorne, Susan (2004) 'The political uses of obscurantism: Gender mainstreaming and intersectionality' *Development Bulletin* 89, pp. 87–91. Also online (2009) at <http://www.susanspoliticalblog.blogspot.com.au/2009/10/gender-mainstreaming.html>.

Hawthorne, Susan (2011) 'Capital and the crimes of pornographers: Free to lynch, exploit, rape and torture' in Melinda Tankard Reist and Abigail Bray (eds) *Big Porn Inc: Exposing the Harms of the Global Pornography Industry*. Spinifex Press, North Melbourne, pp. 107–117.

Hawthorne, Susan and Bronwyn Winter (eds) (2002) *September 11, 2001: Feminist Perspectives*. Spinifex Press, North Melbourne.

Hay, Louise L. (1984) *You Can Heal Your Life*. Hays House, Carisbad, CA.

Hikmet, Nâzim (1951) 'A Sad State of Freedom' [poem] Marxists Internet Archive <http://www.marxists.org/subject/art/literature/nazim/sadstate.html> (accessed 21 July 2013).

Himmler, Heinrich (4 October 1943) 'The Poznan speech' The Holocaust History Project <http://www.holocaust-history.org/himmler-poznan/speech-text.shtml> (accessed 21 July 2013).

Hobson, Janell (27 September 2011) 'Should Black women oppose the SlutWalk?' *Ms. Magazine* <http://msmagazine.com/blog/2011/09/27/should-black-women-oppose-the-slutwalk/> (accessed 12 September 2013).

Hopkin, Susan (2002) *Girl Heroes: The New Force in Popular Culture*. Pluto Press, Annandale.

Hunter, Stuart (7 June 2013) 'FBI raid on Deric Lostutter, AKA KYAnonymous, was in connection with Steubenville hack' *Huffington Post* <http://www.huffingtonpost.com/2013/06/07/deric-lostutter-raid-kyanonymous-steubenville_n_3403000.html> (accessed 21 July 2013).

Hyman, Prue (1999) 'Universal basic income' Money! From Madness to Meaning [seminar] <http://www.wairaka.net/ubinz/IR/items/19990320MoneyMadness.html> (accessed 21 July 2013).

It (1990) motion picture, Warner Brothers, USA. Director Tommy Lee Wallace; producers Mark Basino, Allen S. Epstein, Jim Green.

Jabr, Ferris (22 December 2011) 'Fearless youth: Prozac extinguishes anxiety by rejuvenating the brain' *Scientific American* <http://www.scientificamerican.com/article.cfm?id=prozac-extinguishes-anxiety-rejuvenating-brain> (accessed 21 July 2013).

James, E.L. (2012) *Fifty Shades of Grey*. Random House, London.

Joye, Christopher (19 August 2013) 'Richard Armitage: Why the free ride on US must stop' *Financial Review* <http://www.afr.com/p/national/richard_armitage_why_the_free_ride_Ls2RbuicUIrdvWzJgKcM8H> (accessed 19 August 2013).

Kelley, Michael (8 July 2013) 'Part Two of Snowden's *Guardian* interview could rekindle the PRISM 'direct access' debate' *Business Insider* <http://www.businessinsider.com/snowden-says-nsa-has-direct-access-to-tech-companies-2013-7> (accessed 10 September 2013).

Khan, Nighat Said (2004) 'Up against the State: The women's movement in Pakistan and its implications for the global women's movement' in Luciana Ricciutelli, Angela Miles and Margaret McFadden (eds) *Feminist Politics, Activism, and Vision: Local and Global Challenges*. Inanna Publications, Toronto; Zed Books, London, pp. 86–99.

Kilbourne, Jean (1999) *Can't Buy My Love: How Advertising Changes the Way We Think and Feel*. Touchstone, New York and London.

Kill Bill I (2003) motion picture, A Band Apart Productions, Los Angeles. Director Quentin Tarintino; producer Lawrence Bender.

Kill Bill II (2004) motion picture, A Band Apart Productions, Los Angeles. Director Quentin Tarintino; producer Lawrence Bender.

Klein, Naomi (2007) *The Shock Doctrine: The Rise of Disaster Capitalism*. Metropolitan Books, New York.

Klein, Renate, Janice G. Raymond and Lynette J. Dumble (1991/2013) *RU 486: Misconceptions, Myths and Morals*. Spinifex Press, North Melbourne.

Kramer, Heinrich and James Sprenger (1971) *The Malleus Maleficarum*. Dover Editions, New York.

Kramer, Peter D. (1997) *Listening to Prozac*. Penguin Books, New York.

La Femme Nikita (1990) motion picture, distributed by Gaumont, France. Director and producer Luc Besson.

Lake, Celine and Kellyanne Conway (2005) *What Women Really Want*. Simon & Schuster, New York.

Levi, Primo (2003) *The Drowned and the Saved*, trans. Raymond Rosenthal; intro. Paul Bailey. Abacas, St Ives.

Levi, Primo (2011) [First published 1958, Italy] *If This Is a Man / The Truce*, trans. Stuart Woolf; intro. Paul Bailey. Penguin Books, St Ives.

Lewis, Helen (3 November 2011) '"You should have your tongue ripped out": The reality of sexist abuse online. Female bloggers speak out about misogynist comments, rape threats and death threats' *The New Statesman* <http://www.newstatesman.com/blogs/helen-lewis-hasteley/2011/11/comments-rape-abuse-women> (accessed 21 July 2013).

Lieb, Klaus, Mary C. Zanarini, Christian Schmahl, Marsha M. Linehan, Martin Bohus (2004) 'Borderline personality disorder' *Lancet* 364, pp. 453–461.

Lillington, Catherine (18 June 2013) 'Witnesses tells of their shock after woman plunges to her death from car park roof' *Birmingham Mail* <http://www.birminghammail.co.uk/news/local-news/witnesses-tell-shock-after-woman-4417272> (accessed 21 July 2013).

Lollar, Cortney (2012) 'Child pornography and the restitution revolution' *Journal of Criminal Law and Criminology*, Washington University, St. Louis, Legal Studies Research Paper No. 12-08-02. Available at: <http://ssrn.com/abstract=2123527>.

Loyd, Elizabeth (2005) *The Case of the Female Orgasm*. Harvard University Press, Harvard MA.

Lutz, Catherine (2002) *The Homefront: A Military City and the American 20th Century*. Beacon Press, Boston.

Lutz, Catherine (ed.) (2009) *The Bases of Empire: The Global Struggle against U.S. Military Posts*. New York University Press, New York.

MacKinnon, Catharine A. (2007) *Are Women Human?: And Other International Dialogues*. Harvard University Press, Harvard MA.

MacLean, Nancy (2002) 'Postwar women's history: The "second wave" or the end of the family wage?' in Jean-Christophe Agnew and Roy Rosenzweig (eds) *A Companion to Post-1945 America*. Blackwell Publishers, Malden MA, pp. 235–259.

Mama, Amina (2012) 'Beyond survival: Militarism, equality and women's security' Lecture for the 10th Anniversary of the Prince Claus Foundation <http://www.iss.nl/fileadmin/ASSETS/iss/Documents/Academic_publications/3_mama.pdf> (accessed 20 August 2013).

Mama, Amina (30 May 2013) 'Challenging militarized masculinities' <http://www.opendemocracy.net/5050/amina-mama/challenging-militarized-masculinities> (accessed 20 August 2013).

McDonough, Katie (7 April 2013) 'I'm not a feminist, but …' *Salon* <http://www.salon.com/2013/04/06/im_not_a_feminist_but/> (accessed 14 August 2013).

McEwan, Melissa (9 October 2009) 'Rape culture 101' Shakesville <http://www.shakesville.com/2009/10/rape-culture-101.html> (accessed 21 July 2013).

McGuigan, Jim (2009) *Cool Capitalism*. Pluto Press, London and New York.

McLellan, Betty (1995) *Help! I'm Living with a Man Boy*. Spinifex Press, North Melbourne.

McLellan, Betty (2010) *Unspeakable: A Feminist Ethic of Speech*. OtherWise Publications, Townsville.

McRobbie, Angela (2009) *The Aftermath of Feminism: Gender, Culture and Social Change*. Sage Publications, London.

Merritt, Chris and Patricia Karvelas (10 November 2010) 'Safety first in Gillard's Family Law changes' The Family Law Directory <http://www.thefamilylawdirectory.com.au/article/safety-first-in-gillards-family-law-changes.html> (accessed 16 August 2013).

Mies, Maria (1982/2012) *The Lace Makers of Narsapur*. Spinifex Press, North Melbourne.

Mies, Maria (1986/1998) *Patriarchy and Accumulation on a World Scale: Women in the International Division of Labour*. Zed Books, London; Spinifex Press, North Melbourne.

Mies, Maria (2010) *The Village and the World: My Life, Our Times*. Spinifex Press, North Melbourne.

Miller, Audrey K., E.J. Canales, A.M. Amacker, T.L. Backstrom and C.A. Gidycz (2011) 'Stigma-threat motivated nondisclosure of sexual assault and sexual revictimization: A prospective analysis' *Psychology of Women Quarterly* 35 (1), pp. 119–128.

Mink, Gwendolyn (2001) 'Feminism today: An interview with Gwendolyn Mink' *New Politics* 8 (31), pp. 1–9.

Morris, Nigel (10 January 2013) '100,000 assaults. 1,000 rapists sentenced' *The Independent* <http://www.independent.co.uk/news/uk/crime/100000-assaults-1000-rapists-sentenced-shockingly-low-conviction-rates-revealed-8446058.html> (accessed 12 August 2013).

Mr and Mrs Smith (2005) motion picture, 20th Century Fox, USA. Director Doug Liman; producer Akiva Goldsman.

Oakley, Ann (1976) *Housewife*. Penguin Books, Aylesbury.

Orwell, George (1949/1981) *Nineteen Eighty-Four*. Penguin Books, Harmondsworth.

Parks, Penny (1990) *Rescuing the 'Inner Child': Therapy for Adults Sexually Abused as Children*. Souvenir Press, London.

Penny, Laurie (4 June 2012) '*Game of Thrones* and the good ruler complex' *New Statesman* <http://www.newstatesman.com/blogs/tv-and-radio/2012/06/game-thrones-and-good-ruler-complex> (accessed 12 August 2013).

Petrie, Andrea and Michelle Griffin (17 August 2011) 'The kids are not all right' *The Age* <http://www.theage.com.au/national/the-kids-are-not-all-right-20110816-1iw7l.html> (accessed 15 August 2013).

Pichler, Pia and Jennifer Coates (eds) (2011) *Language and Gender: A Reader*. Wiley-Blackwell, London.

Pierce, Charles P. (9 April 2012) 'The legacy of "welfare reform" and a poverty of ideas' *Esquire* <http://www.esquire.com/blogs/politics/welfare-reform-revisited-7949859> (accessed 21 July 2013).

Piercy, Marge (1979/1985) *Woman on the Edge of Time*. Women's Press, London.

Pittaway, Nigel (3 May 2013) 'Australia sticks with JSF, will buy Growlers, new subs' *Defense News* <http://www.defensenews.com/article/20130503/DEFREG03/305030014/Australia-Sticks-JSF-Will-Buy-Growlers-New-Subs> (accessed 20 August 2013).

Power, Nina (2009) *One Dimensional Woman*. Zero Books, Winchester and Washington.

Radloff, Lenore (1975) 'Sex differences in depression: The effects of occupation and marital status' *Sex Roles* 1 (3), pp. 249–265.

Rettman, Andrew (7 March 2012) 'EU figures show crisis-busting arms sales to Greece' *EUobserver.com* <http://euobserver.com/defence/115513> (accessed 21 July 2013).

Rocheron, Yvette (2009) *Double Crossings*. Matador, Kibworth Beauchamp.

Rose, Steve (15 September 2011) '*Cannibal Holocaust*: "Keep filming! Kill more people!"' *The Guardian* <http://www.theguardian.com/film/2011/sep/15/cannibal-holocaust> (accessed 6 August 2013).

Rosenfeld, Diane L. (2011) 'Who are you calling a "ho"?: Challenging the porn culture on campus' in Melinda Tankard Reist and Abigail Bray (eds) *Big Porn Inc: Exposing the Harms of the Global Pornography Industry*. Spinifex Press, North Melbourne, pp. 41–52.

Rush, Florence (1980) *The Best Kept Secret: Sexual Abuse of Children*. McGraw-Hill, New York.

Salek, Christine (2013) 'Nova-Scotia girl raped, bullied and commits suicide' <http://www.policymic.com/articles/33989/rehtaeh-parsons-nova-scotia-girl-raped-bullied-and-commits-suicide> (accessed 15 August 2013).

Salt (2010) motion picture, di Bonaventura Pictures, USA. Director Philip Noyce; producer Lorenzo di Bonaventura.

Schwartz, Mattathias (3 August 2008) 'The trolls among us' *The New York Times* <http://www.nytimes.com/2008/08/03/magazine/03trolls-t.html?pagewanted=all&_r=1&> (accessed 8 August 2013).

Shaw, Clare and Gillian Proctor (2005) 'Women at the Margins: A critique of Borderline Personality Disorder' *Feminism & Psychology* 15 (4), pp. 483–490.

Simoni-Wastila, Linda (2000) 'The use of abusable prescription drugs: The role of gender' *Journal of Women's Health and Gender-Based Medicine* 9

(2), pp. 289–297 <http://core.ecu.edu/soci/vanwilligenm/wastila.pdf> (accessed 28 August 2013).

Skyfall (2012) motion picture, Columbia Pictures, USA. Director Sam Mendes; producer Michael G. Wilson.

Slijper, Frank (14 April 2013) 'Guns, debt and corruption: Military spending and the EU crisis' [report], Transnational Institute, Washington DC <http://www.tni.org/briefing/guns-debt-corruption>.

Smart, Carol, Bren Neale and Amanda Wade (2001) *The Changing Experience of Childhood: Families and Divorce*. Blackwell, Maiden, MA.

Smith, Anna Marie (20 December 2010) 'Neo-eugenics: A feminist critique of Agamben' *Occasion: Interdisciplinary Studies in the Humanities* vol. 2 <http://occasion.stanford.edu/node/59> (accessed 21 July 2013).

Smith, Helena (20 April 2012) 'German "hypocrisy" over Greek military spending has critics up in arms' *The Guardian* <http://www.theguardian.com/world/2012/apr/19/greece-military-spending-debt-crisis>.

Snuff (1976) motion picture, distributor Alan Shakleton. Directors Michael Findlay, Roberta Findlay; producers Alan Shakleton, Jack Findlay.

Snyder, Bethany (2005) 'The welfare of feminism: Struggle in the midst of reform' Center on Women and Public Policy Cast Study Program, Humphrey Institute of Public Affairs, University of Minnesota, Minneapolis <http://www.hhh.umn.edu/centers/wpp/pdf/case_studies/welfare_of_feminism/welfare_case.pdf> (accessed 21 July 2013).

Solanas, Valerie (1981) *SCUM Manifesto*. Matriarchy Study Group, London.

Spender, Dale (1984) *Man Made Language*. Routledge and Kegan Paul, London.

Stein, Gertrude (1927/2012) 'Patriarchal Poetry' in 'Gertrude Stein: 31 Poems' <http://www.poemhunter.com/i/ebooks/pdf/gertrude_stein_2012_6.pdf> (accessed 23 July 2013).

Steinem, Gloria (1993) *Revolution from Within: A Book of Self-Esteem*. Little, Brown and Company, USA.

Stockholm International Peace Research Institute (n.d.) 'Transparency and accountability in military spending and procurement' <http://www.sipri.org/research/armaments/milex/transparency> (accessed 21 July 2013).

Stoppard, Janet M. (2000) *Understanding Depression: Feminist Social Constructionist Approaches*. Routledge, New York.

Suarez, Eliana and Tahany M. Gadalla (2010) 'Stop blaming the victim: A meta-analysis on rape myths' *Journal of Interpersonal Violence* 25 (11), pp. 2,010–2,035.

Taylor, S. Caroline (2004) *Court Licensed Abuse*. Peter Lang, New York.

Taylor, S. Caroline (forthcoming) *Social Death*. Spinifex Press, North Melbourne.

Temkin, Jennifer (2002) *Rape and the Legal Process*. Oxford University Press, Oxford.

The Matrix (1999) motion picture, Warner Brothers Pictures, USA/Australia. Writers/directors the Wachowski Brothers; producer Joel Silver.

The Telegraph (23 November 2010) 'Attractiveness is all in tilt of the head' <http://www.telegraph.co.uk/women/sex/8153855/Attractiveness-is-all-in-tilt-of-the-head.html> (accessed 21 July 2013).

The Quick and the Dead (1995) motion picture, TriStar Pictures, USA. Director Sam Raimi; producer Joshua Donen.

The Secret (2006) motion picture, Prime Time Productions, Australia. Director Drew Heriot; producer Rhonda Byrne, Paul Harrington.

Tobias, Sheila (1984) *What Kinds of Guns are They Buying for Your Butter? A Beginners Guide to Defense, Weaponry, and Military Spending*. Quill, New York.

Tobias, Sheila (1985) 'Towards a feminist analysis of defense spending' *Frontiers* vol. VIII, no. 2, pp. 65–68.

Tolle, Eckhart (1997/2005) *The Power of Now: A Guide to Spiritual Enlightenment*. Hodder Headline, Sydney.

Underbelly (2008) television series, Screentime Pty Ltd, Australia. Written by Greg Haddick, Peter Gawler, Felicity Packard; producers Des Monaghan, Jo Horsburgh.

Varma, Anuji (13 May 2013) 'Suicide tragedy gran "spent winter without heating to save money"' *Birmingham Mail* <http://www.birminghammail.co.uk/news/local-news/solihull-suicide-tragedy-gran-spent-3660813> (accessed 21 July 2013).

Vigarello, Georges (2001) *A History of Rape: Sexual Violence in France from the 16th to the 20th Century*. Blackwell, Cambridge.

Wacquant, Loïc (2009) *Punishing the Poor: The Neoliberal Government of Social Insecurity*. Duke University Press, Durham.

Walton, Alice G. (26 December 2011) 'The perfect marriage: Science begins to explain why antidepressants and talk therapy go hand in hand' *Forbes* <http://www.forbes.com/sites/alicegwalton/2011/12/26/the-perfect-marriage-science-begins-to-explain-why-antidepressants-and-talk-therapy-go-hand-in-hand> (accessed 21 July 2013).

Wattles, Wallace D. (1910/2006) *The Science of Getting Rich*. Elizabeth Towne Company New York; republished at <http://images.thesecret.tv/The-Science-of-Getting-Rich.pdf> (accessed 26 July 2013).

Webber, Christine and David Delvin (2011) 'Are you having trouble reaching an orgasm? A guide for women' NetDoctor <http://www.

netdoctor.co.uk/sex_relationships/facts/orgasmtrouble.htm> (accessed 21 July 2013).

Williams, Jennie (1999) 'Social inequalities and mental health' in Craig Newnes, Guy Holmes and Cailzie Dunn (eds) *This is Madness: A Critical Look at Psychiatry and the Future of Mental Health Services*. PCCS Books, Ross-on-Wyre, Herefordshire, pp. 29–50.

Wittig, Monique (1972) *Les Guérillères*, trans. David Le Vay. Pan Books, London.

Wolf, Naomi (October 2012) 'Amanda Todd suicide and social media's sexualisation of youth' *The Guardian* <http://www.theguardian.com/commentisfree/2012/oct/26/amanda-todd-suicide-social-media-sexualisation> (accessed 6 August 2013).

World Health Organisation (2012) 'Gender Disparities in Mental Health' Department of Mental Health and Substance Dependence <http://www.who.int/mental_health/media/en/242.pdf> (accessed 21 July 2013).

Wurtzel, Elizabeth (1999) *Bitch: In Praise of Difficult Women*. Quartet Books Limited, Reading.

Young, Iris Marion (2003) 'The logic of masculinist protection: Reflections on the current security state' *Signs: Journal of Women in Culture and Society* 29 (1), pp. 1–25.

Zarkov, Dubravka (2001) 'The body of the other man: Sexual violence and the construction of masculinity, sexuality and ethnicity in Croatian media' in Caroline O.N. Moser and Fiona C. Clark (eds) *Victims, Perpetrators or Actors? Gender, Armed Conflict and Political Violence*. Zed Books, London and New York, pp. 69–82.

Zarkov, Dubravka (ed.) (2008) *Gender, Violent Conflict and Development*. Zubaan Books, New Delhi.

Index

If you would like to know more about Spinifex Press
write for a free catalogue or visit our website.

SPINIFEX PRESS
PO Box 212 North Melbourne
Victoria 3051 Australia
www.spinifexpress.com.au